Leading Insights

Artificial Intelligence

© 2024 by the Association of Christian Schools International

All rights reserved. No portion of this book may be reproduced, stored in a retrieval system, or transmitted, in any form or by any means—mechanical, photocopying, recording, or otherwise—without prior written permission of ACSI.

Views expressed in this book are those of the contributing authors and do not necessarily represent the views of the editors or the position of the Association of Christian Schools International.

Unless otherwise indicated, scripture quotations are from the ESV® Bible (The Holy Bible, English Standard Version®), copyright © 2001 by Crossway Bibles, a publishing ministry of Good News Publishers. Used by permission. All rights reserved.

Revised Standard Version of the Bible, copyright © 1946, 1952, and 1971 the Division of Christian Education of the National Council of the Churches of Christ in the United States of America. Used by permission. All rights reserved.

Printed in the United States of America
29 28 27 26 25 24   1 2 3 4 5 6

Edited by Swaner, Lynn E.
ACSI Leading Insights: Artificial Intelligence
  ISBN 978-1-58331-568-2
  eISBN 978-1-58331-569-9
Catalog#: LD01003
        eLD01003
Designer: Patrick Flowers
Cover design: Patrick Flowers

Association of Christian Schools International
PO Box 62249 • Colorado Springs, CO 80962
800.367.0798 • www.acsi.org

CONTENTS

Introduction: Framing the AI Question 4
    Lynn E. Swaner, Series Editor

PART I – Philosophy and Research

1. AI in Education: Villain, Savior, or Something Else?
    Derek C. Schuurman 10

2. A Biblical Framework for Understanding and Responding to AI
    Dave Mulder 17

3. The State of AI in Christian Schools: Findings from Research
    Lynn E. Swaner and Rian Djita 31

PART II – Christian School Perspectives

4. The Head of School Perspective
    Scott Harsh 48

5. The Teacher Perspective
    Paul Matthews 57

6. The Student Perspective
    Lynn E. Swaner and Derek Wilson 71

PART III – Frameworks for Practice

7. A Framework for Technology Integration in Christian Schools
    Shaun Brooker 83

8. Digital Well-Being and the Christian School
    Christina Crook 94

References 103

About the Authors 108

Introduction: Framing the AI Question[1]
Lynn E. Swaner, Series Editor

Artificial intelligence (AI) is far from new. It is already embedded in existing technologies like smartphone speech-to-text, digital assistants like Siri or Alexa, and GPS-enabled maps or routing apps. However, it was the launch of ChatGPT in November 2022 that brought widespread awareness of AI's potential for the educational sector. This was largely because ChatGPT was the first AI tool that successfully "positioned itself as a disruptive technology that is revolutionising the way students are taught, promoted, and supported in academic environments" (Montenegro-Rueda 2023, 2).

ChatGPT and similar tools are unlike previous AI applications in at least two significant ways. First, they are generative, meaning they use large language models (LLMs) to create new content (such as text or images) based on patterns present in the data they draw from. Second, chatbot tools are applications designed to simulate conversation with human users, typically through text-based interfaces. These tools use various techniques including rule-based systems, machine-learning algorithms, and natural language processing (NLP) to understand user input and generate appropriate responses.[2]

Put simply, these tools are conversational as they draw on nearly limitless data and easily perform academic tasks such as writing essays or providing answers to homework questions. These capabilities imbue the tools with the potential to affect education in significant if not radical ways. Educators around the world reacted to ChatGPT's launch with a range of responses, from implementing bans and installing detection software to embracing ChatGPT and similar tools in day-to-day teaching and learning (Gordon 2023).

Increasing educational effectiveness should be a perennial aim in schools, and AI holds promise for achieving this end. However, for

---

1 Portions of this chapter first appeared as part of a report co-published by ACSI and Cardus (Swaner and Djita 2024).

2 Throughout this chapter, "AI," "ChatGPT," and "chatbots" are used interchangeably to refer to this new class of AI tools that are generative, work off of LLMs, and are conversational (use NLP).

Introduction: Framing the AI Question

Christian schools, the question of whether to adopt AI in practice is not just one of utility. In *A Christian Field Guide to Technology for Engineers and Designers*, Brue, Schuurman, and VanderLeest (2022) describe "the ultimate and proper goal for technology—to help us be more fully human in relationship to each other and to God" (11). To be sure, the question of how to realize this goal—along with deciding whether and how to adopt new AI technologies in Christian schools—is a complex one.

Three lenses for thinking about AI in Christian schools can assist in catalyzing conversations. While these lenses are non-discrete and overlapping, they can be used together to frame discussions and planning around AI. These three lenses—the *use* lens, the *human* lens, and the *mission* lens—are described below, along with suggested reflection questions that leaders, teachers, students, and the school community together can use as they consider the challenges and opportunities posed by AI.

The Use Lens

The first lens to be considered is that of use. All industries, whether education, law, medicine, insurance, or others, are faced with new AI-driven or AI-supported technologies that are affecting their current work and will be shaping their fields for the future. This lens is often referred to in terms of developing "use cases" for these technologies, with an eye toward how they can help to improve performance in the industry (as mentioned earlier, the current use case discussion in education mostly centers around ChatGPT and related tools).

Employing the *use* lens, Christian schools can consider the following questions:
- As a staff, how can we increase our knowledge around AI (through readings, trainings, conferences, certificate programs, etc.)?
- Can we create small-scale experiments or pilots using AI in teaching and learning, from which we can learn without significant risk?
- How can we network with other schools to identify use cases or to collaborate on AI experiments or pilots?

- How can we effectively engage with stakeholders (leaders, teachers, parents, students, others) in discussions and decisions around the use of AI, whether through a task force or other method?

The Human Lens

Many theologians, public intellectuals, technologists, and ethicists are concerned with the impact of AI on humanity. This second *human* lens centers on the practical yet profound question of how AI will shape human nature and human experiences writ large. Fundamental to answering this question is one's view of what it means to be human, from which flows one's ethical reasoning about technology. John C. Lennox, Oxford professor and author of *2084: Artificial Intelligence and the Future of Humanity*, makes the argument that while most technologies in and of themselves are values-neutral, the human question (of how humans use technology) is what imbues technological trajectories with an ethical dimension. As Lennox (2020) writes, "Of course, experience tells us that most technological advances are likely to have both an upside and a downside …. It is the same with AI. There are many valuable positive developments, and there are some very alarming negative aspects that demand close ethical attention" (54). Thus, while connected to the *use* lens, the *human* lens goes a step further to consider the "why" and not just the "how" or "what" of AI.

Using a *human* lens, Christian schools can consider the following questions:
- What is our theological framework at our school for understanding the nature of humans (for example, as created in God's image), and what are the implications of that framework for understanding human inventions and advances (like AI)?
- What is our educational purpose or philosophy? How are we trying to form our students as human persons? How might the use of AI in our schools enhance or detract from this purpose?
- How do we address ethical thinking at our school, especially when it comes to complex issues in society (including those around technology)?
- Do we offer students opportunities to wrestle with contemporary ethical issues (i.e., through reading, considering opposing viewpoints,

Introduction: Framing the AI Question

debating)? What training and support does our faculty need to help our students do this well?

The Mission Lens

People from any faith background or none can engage with questions around AI from the use or human lenses. But the question of how AI can be viewed through the lens of Christian mission is, of course, of importance to Christians inhabiting this moment in human history. Both the Great Commission (Matthew 28:16–20) and Great Commandment (Matthew 22:34–40) have implications for the use of any technology: They lead Christians to ask whether (and if so, how) AI can help spread the gospel, make disciples, and better love and serve their neighbors. This is the latest in a long line of similar questions regarding new technologies, similar questions that date at least as far back to the fifteenth century when Christians considered uses for the printing press (with the result that from the Gutenberg Bible to today, the Bible is the most widely printed book in human history). This third lens certainly overlaps with the first and second, and while Christians can and should consider both, they have a unique obligation to pay attention to this lens as well.

Using a *mission* lens, Christian schools can consider the following questions:

- What is our school's theological view of how Christians should engage the world? How does that view inform teaching, learning, and discipleship at our school?
- Given this theological view, along with our school's mission, how can we evaluate the potential of AI for our school—including whether and how AI can be used to nurture Christian beliefs and values, as well as serve others?
- How might our school winsomely engage faculty, parents, students, or other constituents who hold different theological views of AI?
- What resources can we draw on (books, speakers, webinars) that address AI from a distinctly Christian view?

To help Christian schools address this last question, we have developed the monograph that you now hold. This monograph is divided into three sections: "Philosophy and Research," "Christian School Perspectives," and "Frameworks for Practice." In the first section, authors describe and define AI and its potential for education (chapter 1), present a biblical framework for understanding and responding to AI in the Christian school (chapter 2), and provide a snapshot of AI use across the Christian school sector (chapter 3). In the second section, "Christian School Perspectives," readers will gain insights from a head of school who is leading AI implementation at the middle and high school levels (chapter 4), a Christian school teacher and tech entrepreneur who discusses AI adoption in the classroom (chapter 5), and a focus group of high school students who share their experiences with AI (chapter 6). In the final part of the monograph, "Frameworks for Practice," authors provide a framework for adopting new technology in the Christian school (chapter 7) and suggest ways to consider digital well-being within the Christian school setting (chapter 8).

While AI may differ in significant and potentially profound ways from technologies that have preceded it, Christian school educators can take encouragement in remembering—as well as applying learnings from—previous waves of technological change they have navigated. When it comes to deciding whether or how to engage AI, they will need thoughtfulness and intentionality to chart a deliberate course into the future. We hope and pray this monograph will be a helpful resource along the journey.

Part I:
Philosophy and Research

AI in Education:
Villain, Savior, or Something Else?[1]

Derek C. Schuurman, *Calvin University*

When I was a teenager, I purchased an early personal computer called a Timex Sinclair ZX-81 with money I had earned from my paper route. I was amazed at how computer programs enabled me to build "castles in the air ... creating by exertion of the imagination" (Brooks 1995, 7). What started as a hobby later developed into a vocation as I worked in industry as an engineer and later pursued graduate work in the field of robotics and computer vision.

As I pursued my graduate studies years ago, I found myself attracted to newer machine-learning methods that were being used in computer vision (Fortuna et al. 2002). I recall being astounded at the profound elegance of "training" a computer with a set of example images and then observing how well it could identify new images that were not part of the original training set. Even those early machine-learning techniques seemed magical.

Two things became apparent to me in the following years. First, the technology amplified opportunities to do good as well as to do harm. Already as a grad student, I had observed many research efforts being directed toward face recognition—an intriguing and challenging technical problem that had pitfalls for misuse and a myriad of privacy issues. I consciously chose a research direction that I felt was a more redeeming application of machine learning, such as automating the visual sorting of recyclable goods (House et al. 2011). I later recognized this approach as illustrating the theological notion of *structure* and *direction*: The possibility for machine learning is rooted in the *structure* of God's good creation, and *direction* refers to how we unfold this technology in either obedience or disobedience to God (Wolters 2005).

---

[1] Portions of this chapter first appeared in the following articles by the same author: "ChatGPT and the Rise of AI", Christian Scholar's Review blog, January 20, 2023 (https://christianscholars.com/chatgpt-and-the-rise-of-ai/); "AI and Truth in a Post-Epistemic World", Christian Scholar's Review blog, February 27, 2024 (https://christianscholars.com/ai-and-truth-in-a-post-epistemic-world/); and "AI and Truth", Christian Courier, December 4, 2023, p. 20 (https://www.christiancourier.ca/ai-and-truth/).

The second thing that became apparent to me was that AI was developing faster than many of us would have predicted. As an engineering grad student some twenty years ago, I would have scoffed at the notion of an autonomous car; the computer vision challenges were simply too great in unstructured and unpredictable environments. However, within the decade, Google successfully demonstrated a self-driving car.[2] In the words often attributed to Yogi Berra, "It's tough to make predictions, especially about the future"—even for those who are developing technology.

One of the latest developments to catch widespread attention has been ChatGPT, a chatbot developed by OpenAI. ChatGPT relies on a large language model (LLM) that generates "statistically likely continuations of word sequences" to interact with a user by responding to questions and replying to prompts (Shanahan 2024). While some of the responses are amusing or simply wrong, the results are frequently astonishing, providing surprisingly coherent and cogent responses to a wide variety of prompts, including composing poems, stories, sermons, and essays. Unlike the modest amount of training data I used in my graduate work, ChatGPT-3 used 570 gigabytes of example documents (Tamkin et al. 2021). These LLMs demonstrate "that extraordinary and unexpected capabilities emerge when big enough models are trained on very large quantities of textual data" (Shanahan 2024, 73).

The results have been so remarkable it has led to speculations that essay writing is obsolete and has raised uncertainty about the future of many skilled jobs.[3] Indeed, computer programmers may be programming themselves out of a job. A tool called GitHub Copilot takes input prompts and generates computer code, leading some to speculate about the end of programming (Ito 2023). While rumors of the demise of writing and of programming are likely exaggerated, there will be definite impacts for education (Dakhel et al. 2022).

---

2 A short history of the Waymo project is available at https://waymo.com/about/#story.

3 For example, see Stephen Marche, "The College Essay is Dead," *The Atlantic*, December 6, 2022, and Paul Krugman, "Does ChatGPT Mean Robots are Coming For the Skilled Jobs?" *The New York Times*, December 6, 2022.

Which Way Is AI Headed?
Some are making dramatic claims about how AI will improve education. In an article titled "Why AI Will Save the World," web pioneer Marc Andreesen predicts, "Every child will have an AI tutor that is infinitely patient, infinitely compassionate, infinitely knowledgeable, infinitely helpful" (2023).

Such optimistic claims are not new. The rise of the World Wide Web came with predictions that it would be "a natural force drawing people into greater world harmony" (Negroponte 1996). As we know, while the web provided unprecedented access to information, it did not lead to greater world harmony. It has often become a medium for misinformation, echo chambers, bullying, and polarization.

Likewise, the development of AI will bring benefits in many areas like medicine, enhanced traffic safety, and environmental monitoring, to name a few. But there will be many pitfalls to address. Eric Horvitz, Microsoft's chief scientific officer, sounded a prophetic alarm about one of those pitfalls. He wrote that AI is moving us closer to a "post-epistemic" world "where fact cannot be distinguished from fiction" (2022). In short, AI will have an impact on how we perceive the truth, and educators will need to take heed.

Horvitz identifies one area in which AI will obfuscate the truth: "deepfakes." Deepfakes use AI to create synthetic videos that can impersonate people. In a famous demonstration, researchers at the University of Washington posted a deepfake video of President Obama, making him say whatever they wanted (Langston 2017). Seeing is no longer believing; "truth" can now be manipulated and fabricated.

Another recent development is "astroturfing"—using AI to generate a fake campaign that gives the illusion of a grassroots movement. AI chatbots can be harnessed to post massive amounts of tailored content on social media with the purpose of capturing attention and manipulating people's opinions. Some predict that astroturfing will increasingly distort truth and reality, a prediction that if realized, would pose a direct threat to democratic societies (Schneier and Sanders 2023).

Another impediment to discerning truth occurs when LLMs generate false information referred to as "hallucinations." This should come as no surprise: By their very architecture, LLMs are "simply a system for haphazardly stitching together sequences of linguistic forms ... without any reference to meaning: a stochastic parrot" (Bender et al. 2021). According to Grady Booch, an IEEE (Institute of Electrical and Electronics Engineers) Fellow and chief scientist for engineering at IBM, "Generative modes are unreliable narrators" that can "generate misinformation at scale," and they are now being "unleashed into the wild by corporations who offer no transparency as to their corpus" (Anderson 2023). According to the research of one company, "A.I. chatbots invent information at least 3 percent of the time, and some as much as 27 percent of the time" (Metz 2023).

Other researchers have begun to recognize that AI chatbots are trained with a particular worldview and users are subject to something called "latent persuasion" (Jakesch et al. 2023). Regular usage of AI chatbots can be like having a Jiminy Cricket on your shoulder, autocompleting your thoughts. Over time, such nudging can shape your opinions without your realizing it. In fact, one startling study demonstrated that increasing use of AI is correlated with a decline in religiosity (Jackson et al. 2023). All of this can lead to a kind of syncretism, in which Christians amalgamate secular ideologies promoted by AI alongside Christian thought.

Discerning a Response to AI

We shape our tools, but our tools can also shape us—including shaping our perception of truth. What follows are three general guidelines for Christian educators as we discern a Christian response to AI.

First, we need to avoid the pitfalls of viewing technology with either too much optimism or with undue pessimism. We must reject a reductionistic worldview that sees everything (including education) as amenable to technical solutions. A trust in technology and progress, sometimes referred to as *technicism*, is essentially a form of idolatry (Schuurman 2013, 60). On the other hand, we should not view technological developments with a despair that they will inevitably threaten humanity. AI is part of the latent potential in creation, and we are called to responsibly unfold its possibilities (Schuurman 2022). Theologian Al Wolters (2005) writes that "the Bible is unique in its uncompromising rejection of all attempts ... to identify part of creation as either the villain or the savior" (61).

Second, rather than focusing on what AI can *do*, we need to start with an ontological question: *How are people distinct from machines?* A common tendency is to anthropomorphize our machines, thereby elevating the status of our machines and, in doing so, reducing the distinctiveness of human beings. "Exchanges with state-of-the-art LLM-based conversational agents, such as ChatGPT, are so convincing, it is hard not to anthropomorphize them," writes Shanahan (2024), but we should "resist the siren call of anthropomorphism" (73, 79).

In *Humans Are Underrated*, Geoff Colvin suggests asking the following question: "What are the activities that we humans, driven by our deepest nature or by the realities of daily life, will simply insist be performed by other humans, regardless of what computers can do?" (2016, 42). Already in the 1960s, the early AI pioneer Joseph Weizenbaum explored the notion of automating psychotherapy with a chatbot named ELIZA. He concluded, "There are limits to what computers ought to be put to do" (1976, 5–6). An AI chatbot or robot should never substitute for the human wisdom and empathy of a caring teacher. Without a biblically informed ontological grounding, we will be susceptible to various reductionistic philosophies like physicalism and Gnosticism (Schuurman 2019, 79). The biblical story is clear that while humans are also creatures, we are uniquely created in the image of God and distinct from machines. The notion of the *imago Dei* endures even as our machines become more capable. Theologian Herman Bavinck argued that "a human being does not *bear* or *have* the image of God, but ... he or she *is* the image of God" (2003, 554, emphases in original).

Third, we need to discern *norms* for the responsible use of AI. The creators of ChatGPT bumped up against the "AI Alignment" problem—the challenge of aligning an AI system with the goals and values of the designers. The developers had to grapple with bias (including racism) in their training set. Technology is not neutral, and neither are the algorithms and the training data used in AI. Consequently, AI systems can perpetuate injustice, a real threat as big data is employed in a wide variety of fields including insurance, policing, marketing, loans, and politics (O'Neil 2016). Furthermore, AI tends to favor efficiency over other normative considerations. The Christian philosopher of technology, Jacques Ellul, warned against the ideology of *technique*, which he defined as the drive for "absolute efficiency" applied to "every field of human activity," including education (1989, xxv). We must resist absolutizing efficiency and instead discern creational norms for AI that include considerations like justice, cultural appropriateness, caring, social norms, stewardship, transparency, and trust (Schuurman 2019, 71–108).

Beginning with Ourselves

How do we discern normative uses for AI in education? It begins with ourselves. Ellul provides general advice in his book, *The Presence of the Kingdom*. He points to Romans 12:2, "Do not be conformed to this world, but be transformed by the renewal of your mind, that by testing you may discern what is the will of God, what is good and acceptable and perfect." Ellul argues that "faith produces a renewal of intelligence" and that it "takes place in Jesus Christ, through the action of the Holy Spirit" (1989, 80–81). Ellul argues that this requires a "new style of life" that includes the "whole of life," from "the way we dress and the food we eat" to how we treat our neighbors (119–122).

In our context, a new style of life might include habits of mind and the cultivation of various intellectual virtues. In his book *Epistemology: Becoming Intellectually Virtuous*, author W. Jay Wood reminds us that "wise persons not only possess knowledge of eternal or ultimate significance but have undertaken to become the kinds of persons who naturally desire and pursue this knowledge" (Wood and Wood 1998, 69). Some counterculturable habits that might help us cultivate wisdom include observing Sabbath and limiting our exposure to the constant stream of AI-driven media.

In the mid-twentieth century, C.S. Lewis described the pitfall of developing a "blindness" to certain truths by reading "only modern books." His advice is "to keep the clean sea breeze of the centuries blowing through our minds" by "reading old books" (2014). In our twenty-first-century era, "modern books" are no longer the issue, but rather "modern media." None of us are immune to the "blindness" that may be caused by misinformation, latent persuasion, and astroturfing. We ought to renew our minds with the clean sea breeze of older books including, of course, the Scriptures.

Charting the Course

Ultimately, appropriate norms should point us toward using AI to open up new possibilities for showing love to our neighbor and caring for the earth and its creatures. Already, AI has shown amazing redemptive applications in medicine, drug discovery, environmental monitoring, wildlife preservation, assisting people with disabilities, and enhancing traffic safety. These are fruitful directions for computer scientists to explore. However, computer scientists will need the help of philosophers, theologians, educators, social scientists, and others in the humanities to help direct technologies like LLMs in normative ways. Christian educators must join the wider conversations around AI and discern its impact on teaching, learning, and advancing truth. We ought to heed the apostle Paul's injunction to "test everything; hold fast what is good" (1 Thessalonians 5:21, RSV).

Frederick Brooks, a respected Christian computer scientist, wrote, "It is time to recognize that the original goals of AI were not merely extremely difficult, they were goals that, although glamorous and motivating, sent the discipline off in the wrong direction" (1995). He advocates for IA (intelligence amplifying) systems over AI, suggesting people and machines will be able to do far more than AI alone. As an example, one of my colleagues at Calvin University has been exploring the use of AI for helping people write better as opposed to writing for them (Arnold 2021). It is my strong sense that such an approach will be the most fruitful in education.

We shape our tools, but our tools can also shape us—including shaping our students and their perception of truth. Despite the possibilities for sinful distortions, AI is part of the exciting possibilities in creation that Christians can help unfold in God-honoring ways. Christians will need to join the wider dialogue surrounding AI, recognizing that AI is neither the villain nor the savior, bringing biblical insights into what it means to be human, and discerning norms for its appropriate use in education.

A Biblical Framework for Understanding and Responding to AI

Dave Mulder, *Dordt University*

This chapter is about developing a biblically informed, theologically sound perspective on what it means to be human in a world where artificial intelligence (AI) seems to be omnipresent and nearly omnipotent. Along the way, we will consider the history of AI, the current state of AI, and a biblical view of AI. However, to land in a place where we have some solid understanding of a biblically informed perspective on the role of technology, we need to begin with our own imaginations.

Beginning with Imagination

Human imagination is powerful. God has created us with incredible abilities to wonder, to be curious, to explore, to desire to understand. Imagination is an essential part of our experience of being human. I think of imagination as our capacity to see beyond "what is" to conceive of "what if?" and this is an amazing aspect of how God has created us to be.

When you hear the word *imagination*, perhaps the first thing that comes to mind for you is a sense of "just pretend." We often think of *imagining* and *pretending* to be synonyms, and indeed, pretending is a work of imagination. But pretending has connotations of things being made-up, or just make-believe. It is important to remember that imagination has other connotations, and that imagination is not part of just childhood.

Reframing imagination as a key part of creating may be helpful. Creation is an important biblical theme. God is, of course, the Creator. But I believe it's worth remembering that we human beings are created in His image. This reality means that we, too, are created to create. My friend and colleague Dr. Justin Bailey invites us to consider "imaginative generativity" as part of the work of creativity. Bailey says, "We use our imaginations to reinterpret and renew cultural materials, playing with possibilities, provoking desire and delight" (2022, 107). Viewed this way, imagination is more an act of creation, rather than "just pretend." Our imaginative capacities are an essential part of our own creative work.

As we move through the world, and as we encounter new and different ideas and experiences, our imaginative capacities help us make sense of these encounters. But perhaps this fact begs a question for us as well: Do our experiences shape our imagination, or does our imagination shape the way we understand our experiences? Which way is it? I suspect that both are true for most of us. Our imaginations *do* impact the way we experience the world, but the things we experience in our lives also might change the shape of our imaginations.

We cannot avoid the fact that replicating human intelligence in non-human devices has a long history in fiction. Proto-robots, automatons, and non-human creatures brought to life through magical means are prevalent in the myths, legends, and folktales of many cultures. Ancient Greek mythology includes tales of Hephaestus creating automatons like Talos to protect people, and Daedalus creating statues that could come to life to serve King Minos. Early Jewish mystical traditions include the legend of the Golem, a huge, humanoid creature made of clay that could protect people in distress and serve them, brought to life by rabbis through magical means. Even the Scarecrow in *The Wizard of Oz* might be considered an attempt to replicate human intelligence ("if I only had a brain").

More recently, many films include robots and artificially intelligent machines, beginning with the humanoid robots in *Metropolis* (from 1927) to Robby the Robot in *Forbidden Planet* (1956), to the lovable droids in *Star Wars* (1977). But these generally positive examples of "intelligent" machines are shown in contrast by HAL 9000, the malfunctioning computer program that derails the mission to Jupiter in *2001: A Space Odyssey* (1968). Suddenly, viewers were given a vision for what risks a malevolent artificial intelligence might enact on human beings—all in the realm of cinematic imagination, of course. The dangers of AI running amok made for fearsome antagonists in the form of artificially intelligent robots and computers for many science fiction films in the 1980s, 1990s, and early 2000s: *TRON*; *Blade Runner*; *The Terminator*; *Robocop*; *The Matrix*; *I, Robot*; and *Wall·E*. The robots we see in these fictional tales might prompt us to wonder about the intelligence of the machines in our real world.

But just how do these cinematic examples translate into reality? That's a bit more complicated. The way AI has been portrayed in media over the years and the way AI (currently) exists aren't necessarily the same thing.

The villainous (or heroic) artificially intelligent agents in the movies seem a long way off from the AI-powered chatbots (e.g., ChatGPT) that have recently become very intriguing to many people. It might then surprise you to see how firmly embedded AI already is in culture today.

A Brief History of AI

Although it might surprise you, in truth, you almost certainly benefit from AI-powered tools on a daily basis already. If you have a smartphone, you probably use autocorrect and predictive text, speech-to-text, facial recognition (perhaps to unlock your phone), and maybe a personal digital assistant (i.e., Siri or Alexa). All of these are AI-powered. Maps and navigation apps use AI to help plot your route. Recommendations on Netflix, Spotify, and all the other streaming platforms you might use are leveraging AI to help make those suggestions. The algorithms powering your search engine are AI-based. Even grammar-check and spell-check in your word processor are driven by AI. So, while we might feel like AI has come out of nowhere and crashed onto the scene, the reality is that most of us have been quietly benefiting from artificial intelligence in our digital devices for years already.

Let's take a brief look at a bit of the history of artificial intelligence research. Explorations in real-life AI couldn't really begin until the age of computers. Early computing theorists like Alan Turing argued that computers could be taught to "think," and this led to what has been dubbed the Turing Test for artificially intelligent computer systems: Basically, if a person were asking questions of a computer and a human and could not, from the answers received, distinguish which was the human, then that computer could be considered "intelligent." Part of the problem early on, however, was that sufficiently powerful computers to even contemplate using as candidates for the Turing Test were incredibly expensive. It was some time before the development of microprocessors in the 1970s could make powerful computers more affordable.

The 1970s and 1980s were heady times for computer scientists, as computers became cheaper and more powerful at an exponential rate. Perhaps you've heard of Moore's Law, which was formulated by Gordon Moore, one of the founders of Intel (a leading manufacturer of integrated circuits and microprocessors—which are what make modern computers possible). In 1965, Moore suggested that the number of transistors (the tiny digital switches that make computers actually "work") in an integrated circuit would double every two years—meaning that computers would continue to become predictably more powerful (and more economical) with each iteration. This prediction basically held true until around 2010, which is remarkable! Computers continued to become smaller, more powerful, and cheaper throughout that time. And it's not that computer engineers don't continue to develop and refine their designs today; they certainly do. It's more that there is a finite, physical limit to just how small transistors can be, and this has limited the continued shrinking of the size of computer components.

This development of smaller, more powerful, more affordable computers has had a direct impact on what kinds of things computer scientists were able to do with computers, including developments in processing language, computer vision, and parallel processing (which further sped up the calculations computers were able to conduct). Perhaps it's no wonder that computer scientist Marvin Minsky boldly predicted in an article in *Life* magazine in 1970, "In three to eight years we will have a machine with the general intelligence of an average human being" (Darrach 1970, 58B–68B). While Minsky was almost certainly off on the timeline, perhaps we have reached the point where computers do seem able to pass the Turing Test. IBM's Deep Blue computer beat chess grandmaster Garry Kasparov in a chess match in 1997. Microsoft developed speech recognition software called Dragon that could accurately understand human speech and respond appropriately in the late 1990s. And Kismet, a robot developed at MIT, was taught how to recognize—and imitate—human emotions in the 1990s as well.

When we hear about these kinds of developments, it might prompt a whole range of responses from awe, to fear, to confusion. I think all of these are appropriate responses. But it's intriguing to hear futurists like Ray Kurzweil make predictions that computers will surpass human intelligence; this is an event that he has named "the Singularity." Kurzweil has been forecasting the Singularity since the late 1990s as an event that is not an "if" but a "when." In an interview in 2016, Kurzweil suggested that computers will reach human levels of intelligence as demonstrated by a real sense of humor and the capacity to love by 2029 (Pagliery and King 2016). Some people might celebrate this, others might react with horror, or maybe some kind of emotion in between—perhaps you find yourself here as well.

I am not convinced that computers have the actual capacity to love. We should continue to ask this question: Although our machines are powerful tools, at the fundamental level, what are computers? They are very sophisticated calculators. At their root, all computers do is use an immensely large collection of very, very tiny switches to make mathematical calculations. And while different kinds of computers have very different architectures, they don't really function much like human brains at all. I think we need to be very careful about making strong comparisons between human brains and computer processors—and it's easy to fall into this trap in both directions: It's easy to talk about computers "thinking," and it's easy to talk about human brains as though they are just "processing information."[1] In our media-saturated imaginations, we might begin to equate the intelligence of the machine to human intellectual capacities. But this is problematic! Human intelligence is, at this point, still a fundamentally different thing than what the machines are able to do.

AI Today: Chatbots, LLMs, and Beyond

Let's turn our attention to the current situation of artificial intelligence. In particular, let's pay attention to how our imaginations inform the way we perceive the role of technology in society today. If you have experimented with an AI chatbot like ChatGPT, I suspect that you—like me—have been surprised, impressed, or even a little bemused by the output. My imagination, which has been so thoroughly shaped by my experiences with other technologies as well as books and films, causes me to wonder about the future of a world where such technologies exist—both the potential benefits and the very real downsides. To use our imaginations a bit more productively, let's take a look at how AI chatbots are developed.

When you hear about the development of AI today, you will surely notice some particular terminology being used to describe programming

---

[1] Sociologist Sherry Turkle explores this idea extensively in her book *Alone Together: Why We Expect More from Technology and Less from Each Other* (Philadelphia: Basic Books, 2012).

for artificial intelligence. *Neural networks, machine learning,* and *natural-language processing* are terms that get thrown around a lot. Neural networks are a particular type of computer architecture that mimics the way connections are set up between neurons in a human brain. Machine learning is a way of programming computers based on massive data sets that train algorithms by pattern recognition. Natural-language processing is a way of programming computers to be able to take normal human language and interpret it into data that the computer can use. When we start thinking about AI chatbots in particular, these terms become important because the input is natural language and the output is language-based, put together by the machine based on the information in the database used to train it.

Most of the powerful computers being used to develop tools like ChatGPT utilize machine learning to develop natural-language processing. ChatGPT is a "large language model" (LLM), which means it is a program (a "model") that was trained on an absolutely gigantic body of text to "understand" human language (English, at least, as well as Spanish, French, German, Portuguese, Italian, Dutch, Russian, Arabic, and Chinese). When a user gives ChatGPT a prompt using normal human language, the AI model generates a response based on its training and the resources it has access to, which is more or less the whole of the World Wide Web as of 2021. This response is generated on the basis of probabilities; the combination of words in the prompt you enter is sort of like planting seeds in the large language model, and these germinate by associations the AI makes between words in the database it was trained on. Words that are often connected by proximity in the database are likely to show up in the resulting text. And the more prompts the chatbot receives from users, the more it can improve the responses it generates, because it is designed to use machine-learning algorithms to keep refining the way it connects information in the database. Responses from early chatbots were looser in terms of the kind of results they generated and weren't always very precise. But chatbots are rapidly developing, and machine learning means they can get better faster. Chatbots' rapid development and machine learning led to some pretty amazing responses to our queries.

If you've played around with an AI chatbot like ChatGPT, the responses can be surprisingly humanlike, so maybe it's no wonder people are wowed—and scared—by the potential of a tool like this. And perhaps this is where our imaginations, which have been formed by portrayals of artificial intelligences in literature and film, begin to make us imagine either the utopian or dystopian implications of such a powerful tool.

In light of this, we need to face the facts of the current situation and check where our imaginations might be running ahead of us. Keep in mind that while tools like AI chatbots are growing in power and capabilities, every tool has limitations as well. For all the wonder we might assign to the response we read blooming out of a query we pose to a large language model like ChatGPT, these results are limited by the (admittedly large) dataset used to train the model. The dataset ChatGPT draws from certainly has biases, blind spots, incomplete information, and even incorrect information included. The old adage in computer science really does hold true: "Garbage in, garbage out." If the data used to train the language model is "garbage," we should be cautious about the results and how much we trust them.

If you are old enough to remember Clippy, the animated AI paperclip that used to be part of Microsoft Word, you perhaps have firsthand experience with a less-than-useful example of how an AI agent can let us down. In a section on the limitations of artificial intelligence in his book *Smarter Than You Think*, Clive Thompson (2013) gives this assessment of Clippy: "Microsoft is still living down its disastrous introduction of Clippy, a ghastly piece of artificial intelligence—I'm using that term very loosely—that would observe people's behavior as they worked on a document and try to burst in, offering 'advice' that tended to be spectacularly worthless" (37). Thompson is generally quite positive about the whole idea of people leveraging the powers of AI, but even in his rosy outlook, he finds examples worth critique. Chatbots certainly can produce useful, valuable responses to our questions and prompts, but it's important for us to remember that we should consider them carefully—just as we would with any other technology.

***Re*-Imagining AI**

In my research into the history of educational technology, this is almost always the reality of the situation: New technologies bring solutions to some problems but are simultaneously the cause of other, new problems. Along these lines, the cultural critic Neil Postman once said, "It is not always clear, at least in the early stages of a technology's intrusion into a culture, who will gain most by it and who will lose most. This is because the changes wrought by technology are subtle if not downright mysterious, one might even say wildly unpredictable" (1993, 12). This unpredictability is often where we find ourselves curiously in over our heads with our own imaginations—we might either imagine a utopia or a dystopia, but the reality is almost always somewhere in between. Rarely are new technologies either the panacea for all our problems or the bogeyman to be banished. The truth is almost always somewhere in the murky middle.

I hope that the ideas in this chapter so far have prompted you toward some metacognition about your own imagination regarding artificial intelligence. What do you believe about AI chatbots? Should their use be encouraged? Shall we hold them at arm's length? Should we unabashedly embrace them? Should we seek to ban them? I believe the way we answer questions like these reveals something important about our own imaginations of what AI is and what it does.

The main thing I want to encourage is that we should carefully consider the pros and cons of implementing them, particularly in educational settings. Perhaps a productive way forward for us is to think about what it means to be human in light of the teachings of Scripture. By doing so, we can *reimagine* the "what is" and the "what if?" of artificial intelligence and other technologies in light of a Christ-centered theological perspective.

A Biblical View

What does it mean to be human? Philosophers, theologians, and everyday people of all stripes and throughout history have grappled with this question and given their own particular answers. The answers we might give to this key question are informed by our worldviews, and in a technological world, we might find ourselves tempted to give an answer rooted in a humanistic, consumeristic, technocratic view of the world. The media forces that are acting on our imaginations, after all, are powerful. But if we intentionally lean into a biblically informed perspective, we can articulate a Christ-centered anthropology that can—and should—inform our imagination of what it means to be human.

For example, if we start at the beginning, we find a very clear and important statement of what it means to be human. Genesis 1:27 (NIV) tells us: "So God created mankind in His own image, in the image of God He created them; male and female He created them." This bold, clear articulation illustrates something essential of what it means to be a human being: *We reflect what God is like.* What an amazing thought! God is the Creator; we image bearers reflect this in our creative capacities. God is love; we image bearers reflect this through our loving actions. God is just; we image bearers reflect this in our works of justice and mercy. God is wise; we image bearers reflect this in our capacity for wisdom and reason. Just as the image you see in the mirror is not *you*, we who bear the image of God are *not God*, but we are able to reflect what God is like.

Moving forward just a few verses in Genesis, we read, "God saw all that He had made, and it was very good" (Genesis 1:31, NIV). Throughout the first chapter of Genesis, we hear the refrain that God's creation is good. And after humans were added to the creation, God declares that the total work is "very good." This is an important reminder: Humans were created *good*. God does not make junk.

That said, it can sometimes be hard to see the goodness, because while human beings were created good, we are now sinful. It is crucial to remember that this is not how things are supposed to be; Genesis 3 tells the story of the Fall, and how Adam and Eve—representatives of the whole human race—turned away from God in disobedience. Through their sin, all of creation was tarnished. Al Wolters (2005) explains the Fall this way, saying:

> We must stress that the Bible teaches plainly that Adam and Eve's fall into sin was not just an isolated act of disobedience, but an event of catastrophic significance for creation as a whole. Not only the whole human race but the whole nonhuman world too was caught up in the train of Adam's failure to heed God's explicit commandment and warning. The effects of sin touch all of creation; no thing is in principle untouched by the corrosive effects of the fall. (53)

Though we can certainly still see the goodness of God's design for creation, the whole of it has been twisted through the effects of sin. What can be done?

Jesus came to save the day; thanks be to God! Jesus certainly came to pay the debt of human sin, but the implications of this salvation are far more than just saving us: His redeeming work breaks sin's hold on all of creation. Jesus' death and resurrection bring healing and restoration for all things. Wolters puts it this way: "Through Christ, God determined to 'reconcile to himself *all things*,' writes Paul (Colossians 1:20).… The scope of redemption is as great as the fall; it embraces creation as a whole" (72, emphasis in original). This is good news. We have the possibility of new life through Jesus Christ, and we have hope that all that seems wrong can—and will—be made right again.

We are living in the in-between times now. Jesus has fought and won the decisive battle at the cross, defeating the power of sin and death and evil. But the war rages on, though the final victory has already been secured. We, the redeemed people Jesus saved, are invited to join in the fight as well.[2] But we should be clear about what this fight looks like: Jesus does not need us. He is God, after all! Rather, He loves us, and invites us to participate in the renewal of all things. This is a crucially important distinction: our "fight" is love, justice, mercy, and kindness—we are fighting for renewal and restoration.

For Christians, these four truths must inform our imagination:
1. God created humans in His image, and God does not make junk—humankind was created good.
2. Human sinfulness brought the painful brokenness that permeates the world.
3. Jesus' death and resurrection heal this brokenness and bring hope that all will be made right.
4. Human beings are invited into the process of working toward the renewal of all things until Jesus comes again.

---

[2] Wolters uses this analogy of wartime between Jesus and the forces of evil—how Jesus has really spelled out their doom and is now moving toward the mopping-up operation to great effect. (See pages 83–86 of *Creation Regained*.)

This is the overarching story of the whole of Scripture, and it tells us who we are and our role in the Story. We are not the Creator, and we are not the Redeemer. We are created, broken, beloved, saved, redeemed, and invited. Knowing this, we can have a better imagination for what we are called to do in this world.

Applying a Biblical View in Practice

Understanding the truth of this biblically informed view of personhood compels us to act in particular ways. As we consider what it means to be a person in a world where AI exists so powerfully and prevalently, we must cling to the truth of what it means to be human. As amazing as our machines may be, they are not created in God's image. If anything, they are created in *our* image, reflecting what we are like—both the good and the sinfulness. In our hubris, we might imagine that the artificial intelligences we create will be all good, but they surely will also be twisted and tainted by sin, as all things in this world are. But here, too, in response to Christ's redemption of us human beings and His invitation to work toward the renewal of all things, perhaps we can direct our imaginative, creative capacities toward wise discernment for the proper role of technology in our lives.

Andy Crouch (2022) has done a marvelous job of encouraging this in his book *The Life We're Looking For: Reclaiming Relationship in a Technological World*. The whole book hinges on his definition of what it means to be human. Crouch uses Jesus' own words when He was asked which of the commandments is the most important: "The most important is, 'Hear, O Israel: The Lord our God, the Lord is one. And you shall love the Lord your God with all your heart and with all your soul and with all your mind and with all your strength.' The second is this: 'You shall love your neighbor as yourself.' There is no other commandment greater than these" (Mark 12:29–31). And from this exposition of the most important commandment, Crouch delivers his definition: "Every human person is a heart-soul-mind-strength complex designed for love" (33). This depiction of what it means to be human has thoroughly captured my imagination, and I hope it captures yours as well. A human being is not a soul without a body. A human being is not a mind without a soul. A human being is not a body without a heart. And a human being is not human without love.

As we think about artificial intelligences, we can see that while these tools are powerful, they are not human. They are tools. Crouch reminds us of the importance of this as well, stating that "there is a difference between 'something' and 'someone' " (28). We must recognize that the digital devices that have become ubiquitous in our cultural context are instruments—powerful tools, certainly—but they cannot truly replicate nor in any meaningful way replace human beings.[3] We must not treat our machines as people any more than we treat people as machines. We must not elevate technological devices to the point that they are "alive enough" that we can imagine them to replace human beings.[4] Our imaginations need redemption just as much as the rest of us, since we are heart-soul-mind-strength complexes designed for love. The way we imagine using contemporary technologies (and the technologies still to be developed) must be informed by and inspired by this biblically informed view of personhood.

A Theology of Educational Technology

We live in a technologically oriented world, and the children we serve in schools are growing up into a world that we can barely even imagine at this point. About a decade ago, I was taking a graduate course that focused on emerging technologies, and in a class discussion, a colleague made an intriguing observation: "The iPad is the worst technology my kids are ever going to use." What he meant by that comment is that with the constant push for technological improvements, the tablets of the early 2010s would almost certainly be considered passé in a relatively short time. In the face of the rush of so many new innovations flying toward us, we can scarcely keep up. Our imaginations run wild with both the promises of technological cure-alls as well as the worries of machine-dominated nightmares.

Building up on the biblically informed anthropology I've laid out in this chapter, I have the beginnings of what I might call a theology of educational technology. I have three ideas I would like to propose that might be useful

---

3 This is the central argument Crouch makes in Chapter 9 of *The Life We're Looking For*, a chapter titled "From Devices to Instruments."

4 This is a key part of Sherry Turkle's argument in *Alone Together*. Chapter 2 uses "Alive Enough" as the title, and herein she explores the ways children—and adults, too—tend to treat robotic toys as if they are alive and have emotions, when they clearly do not.

for Christian educators looking for a systematic approach for determining which technologies to include and how to use them as part of the teaching and learning endeavor. Each of them involves acts of imagination.

First, we must remember that education is more than transmission of information. The technologies we choose might support the sharing out of ideas, but becoming educated is a fuller, richer experience than just downloading the right data. (If that were all education is about, a computer could certainly do that, and perhaps more efficiently than a human teacher.) Instead, we must imagine ways that the technologies we implement will foster the development of people, both individually and as a community. The kind of formation we find in community, with a loving, caring, thoughtful teacher leading the way, is wildly different from the kind of formation we experience in a solo, me-and-my-computer transmission of information. In our theology of educational technology, we should imagine the ways that new tools will support or disrupt the kind of formation we desire in our students and faculty members alike: How will these tools be part of making people more like Jesus?

Second, we should cultivate healthy skepticism about the claims made about technologies that people want to introduce into the teaching and learning endeavor. By "healthy" skepticism, I mean that we should be careful to neither immediately block any innovations nor wholeheartedly embrace novel technologies. God has given us the capacity to discern, and we must do so sharply when it comes to new tools, because we can rarely see the full effects from the outset. Are there questions about how ChatGPT will impact education, both in the short and long term? Absolutely. Becoming an EdTech skeptic means remembering that AI chatbots are almost certainly neither the thing that will save education the way some fanatics describe them nor the end of education as some critics seem to think. The truth is usually somewhere in between these poles.

We need wisdom to find the truth. This is where encouragement from Scripture is needed: "Beloved, do not believe every spirit, but test the spirits to see whether they are from God, for many false prophets have gone out into the world" (1 John 4:1), and "It is my prayer that your love may abound more and more, with knowledge and all discernment, so that you may approve what is excellent, and so be pure and blameless for the day of Christ" (Philippians 1:9–10). We must do this discerning work diligently, testing the spirits of this age, and working out this discernment in a way that demonstrates our love for God and neighbor. We must use our imaginative capacities with wisdom to judge the possibilities and pitfalls of new technologies.

Finally, we must remember the broad arc of the story of Scripture. Remember that God created all things good, and while all things are tainted by sin, Jesus' redeeming work is likewise cosmic in scope. We are eagerly anticipating the renewal of all things when Jesus comes again. But now, consider this: The arc of the Story is one that illustrates technological development. In the beginning, in Genesis, we read of Adam and Eve being carefully placed by their Creator in the Garden (Genesis 2–3). But if we flip to the last pages at the end of the book, we see that the Story does not end with a return to the Garden. Rather, we find ourselves in the City, the New Jerusalem coming out of heaven down to the earth, where the Creator rejoins his people (Revelation 21–22). The move from the Garden to the City demonstrates a progression of technology, and I think this is an important reminder for us. The Story is a dynamic unfolding of creation throughout history. Technological development is not separate from God's plan, nor outside of His sovereignty. We can imagine ways that we can participate in the renewal of all things, even by developing and implementing new technologies.

My hope is that this tentative beginning toward a theology of educational technology can give you the confidence to engage wisely, judge carefully, and discern sharply the appropriate place for new technologies in the sphere of education. Artificial intelligence is here, and we certainly must decide how we will respond to the potential benefits and drawbacks that come with this powerful tool. But I am optimistic that a Christian imagination and a biblically informed view of personhood can guide us to carefully navigate the possible pitfalls, even as we explore the ways we can utilize artificial intelligence for educational advantages.

Philosophy and Research

The State of AI in Christian Schools: Findings from Research

Lynn E. Swaner, *Cardus*, and Rian Djita, *ACSI*[1]

Introduction

The Association of Christian Schools International (ACSI) conducted a member survey in late 2023 regarding AI usage and perceptions. ACSI is the largest Protestant Christian school association with close to 5,500 schools around the world, 2,300 of which are in the United States. ACSI membership is diverse in terms of school size (by enrollment), structure (independent or church-sponsored), admissions practices, and urbanicity.

The results of the survey provide insight into ACSI school policies and give instruction about AI. The survey tells how educators and their schools are using AI in teaching and learning, and it contains educators' perceptions about the benefits, drawbacks, and future of AI in education. This chapter will unpack the survey findings, first to provide a descriptive look at the state of AI adoption in surveyed Christian schools, and second to create a profile of early adopters of AI within these schools.

Survey Methodology

ACSI fielded an electronic survey on AI to member schools in early November 2023 for two weeks. The target participants included school leaders (administrators, heads of school), teachers, and staff. The survey was sent to a total of 16,797 individuals, with 705 responding.[2]

Sample Demographics

The majority of the sample were teachers (57 percent), followed by heads of school (22 percent), administrators (16 percent), and non-teaching staff, including counselors, coaches, and administrative staff (5 percent). Respondents were predominantly female, and the majority of these participants' ages fell in the range of 45–54 years. Among respondents, there was almost an even split between those who had graduated from Christian colleges or universities (49 percent) and those who had graduated from public or private non-sectarian

---

[1] This chapter first appeared as part of a report co-published by ACSI and Cardus (Swaner and Djita 2024).

[2] The invitation was sent to all individuals on two ACSI email marketing lists (one for teachers and one for administrators). The response rate for the survey was 4.2 percent, and the completion rate for those who responded was 70 percent.

colleges or universities (51 percent). Eighty-seven percent of respondents were in the United States, and 13 percent were in thirty-four other countries.

As for school characteristics, 61 percent of the respondents worked at covenantal schools (meaning the school requires parents to be active members of a church and/or to sign a statement of faith upon the admission of their children to the school), 55 percent worked in a school with an enrollment below 250 students, 60 percent worked in a school located in suburban areas, and 38 percent worked in a school in the southern part of the United States. Detailed demographics for the sample are provided in the table below.

Participants' Demographics and Schools' Characteristics

Variable	No. of Respondents	Percentage of Respondents
Roles	706	
Administrator (principals, vice principals, etc.)	116	16%
Head of School (HOS)	153	22%
Teacher	400	57%
Other school staff (athletic coach, counselor, etc.)	37	5%
Gender	479	
Male	179	37%
Female	300	63%
Age	478	
18–24	7	1%
25–34	60	13%
35–44	104	22%
45–54	135	28%
55–64	119	25%
65+	53	11%
Higher education graduates	484	
Christian university / college graduates	238	49%
Non-Christian university / college graduates	246	51%
Type of Christian schools	267	
Covenantal	162	61%
Non-covenantal	105	39%

Variable	No. of Respondents	Percentage of Respondents
Student enrollment	**261**	
10–249 students	118	45%
250–499 students	77	30%
500–1000 students	47	18%
More than 1000 students	19	7%
Accreditation	**635**	
Accredited only by ACSI	537	85%
Accredited by other association and/or ACSI	98	15%
Urbanicity of the school	**646**	
Urban	138	21%
Rural	123	19%
Suburban	385	60%
Region of the school	**574**	
Midwest	121	21%
Northeast	75	13%
South	219	38%
West	158	28%

Data Analysis

Two analytical approaches are used for this chapter. First, descriptive analyses are provided for the survey questions. Following the methodology of a previous Cardus report by Cheng et al. (2022), this first analysis did not control for demographic or school characteristics. Instead, overall individual-level averages were compared among all the respondents. This approach seeks to generate baseline descriptive data. Next, simple regression was used to explore possible relationships among outcome variables, by controlling for respondents' demographic information and school characteristics. While causality cannot be identified through this analysis, it provides a clearer picture of relationships, specifically about respondent characteristics that correlate with higher rates of AI adoption.

Key Findings

This section first provides descriptive results for Christian school educators (administrators and teachers)[3] organized by three themes: (1) educator use of AI; (2) school responses to AI; and (3) educator perceptions related to AI. Then, using findings from regression analysis, correlational data is used to paint a picture of early adopters of AI in these Christian schools.

Educator Use of AI

Overall, the survey data regarding educators' use of AI and related tools suggest that the respondents are in the beginning stages of engaging with AI technology. First, we asked respondents to gauge their level of familiarity with AI. While a majority of educators (50 percent) indicated they were somewhat familiar with AI chatbots and related tools, close to a third (30 percent) were not familiar at all with the technology, and only 20 percent were very or extremely familiar (figure 1).

Figure 1

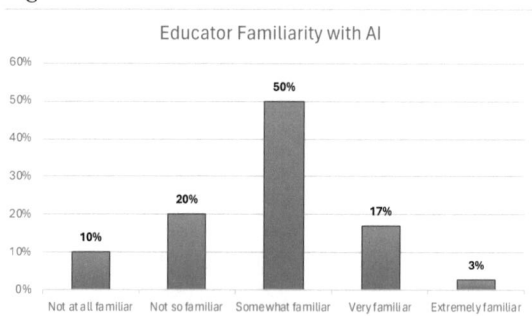

The survey then asked respondents about the frequency with which they use AI at work. Over a third of educators (37 percent) reported that they have never used AI at work, and an additional quarter (25 percent) reported using the technology only rarely. Less than a third (30 percent) reported using AI sometimes, and 8 percent reported using the technology always or usually. Compared with educators' familiarity with AI, the current state of usage among

---

3 Throughout this chapter, where the term "educators" is used, this means that results for administrators and teachers are combined and reported together. We only note differences in respondents (administrators versus teachers) if those differences were greater than 10 percentage points.

Philosophy and Research

Christian school educators skews heavily toward non-use or infrequent use (figure 2).

Figure 2

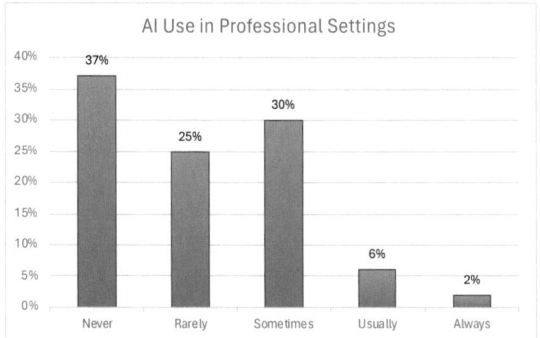

Similar to educators' level of use, their level of confidence with AI also skews toward the low side, with 25 percent of educators reporting being very or extremely confident in using AI chatbots or tech tools effectively (figure 3).

Figure 3

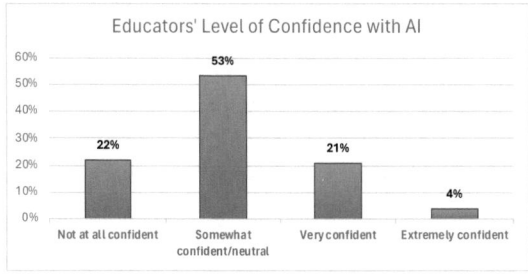

The survey then asked those educators who reported using AI with any frequency in their work (63 percent of the total sample) to indicate the ways in which they use the technology. The top five ways educators report using AI in professional settings are to detect plagiarism (38 percent), find teaching ideas (37 percent) and teaching resources (33 percent), prepare emails (30 percent), and prepare lesson plans (28 percent). Additional AI usage includes developing school resources (28 percent), finding meeting ideas (19 percent), translating materials (17 percent), drafting reports (17 percent), scheduling meetings (15 percent), and grading (14 percent) (figure 4).

Figure 4

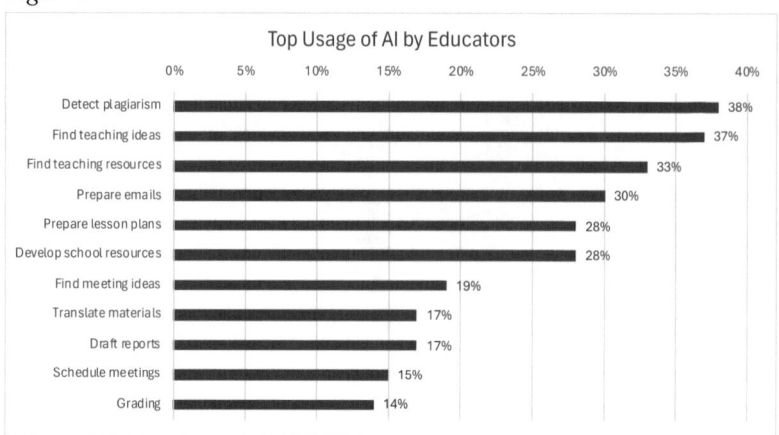

School Responses to AI

In addition to asking about educator use of AI, the survey asked a number of questions about how these educators' schools were responding to the advent of AI technology.[4] About a third (34 percent) of respondents reported that their school was using AI in teaching and learning, and less than a third (31 percent) of schools offer some kind of AI-specific instruction or course for students (figure 5).[5] For the 34 percent of respondents who reported that their schools were incorporating AI in instruction, they indicated that AI incorporation primarily occurs in high school (73 percent), followed by middle school (18 percent), and upper elementary (5 percent). At schools offering some kind of AI-specific instruction or course for students, educators report that the most common topics covered are practical uses of AI (40 percent), ethical implications (36 percent), and theological perspectives (20 percent).

---

[4] The percentages reported here refer to the percentage of educators, not percentage of schools, as the sample potentially included more than one respondent from some of the schools.

[5] For this and other questions related to school use, where noted with an asterisk (*), administrators' responses differed from teachers' by more than 10 percentage points; thus, administrators' responses are provided here with the rationale that they have a better vantage point of schoolwide incorporation of AI than a single classroom teacher.

Figure 5

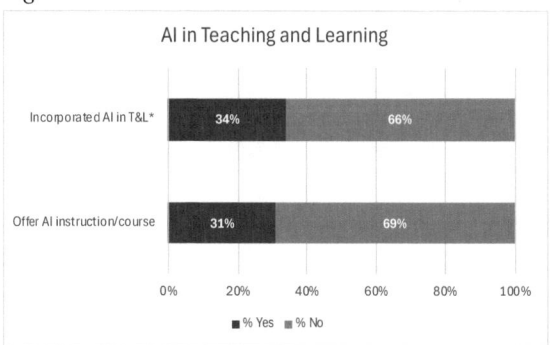

AI in Teaching and Learning

- Incorporated AI in T&L*: 34% Yes, 66% No
- Offer AI instruction/course: 31% Yes, 69% No

At schools incorporating AI in instruction, educators reported the top four uses as (1) automated tasks, such as providing teachers with various prompts for essays or creating lesson plans; (2) new learning tools, such as AI-powered games or other interactive games; (3) adaptive learning, providing students with more or less challenging materials depending on their performance; and (4) personalized learning, in which AI-powered tutoring programs tailor instruction to the individual needs of students (figure 6).

Figure 6

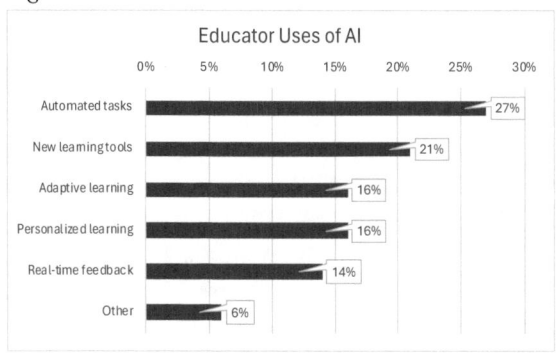

Educator Uses of AI

- Automated tasks: 27%
- New learning tools: 21%
- Adaptive learning: 16%
- Personalized learning: 16%
- Real-time feedback: 14%
- Other: 6%

The survey also asked respondents whether their school has responded to AI by implementing bans or policies, installing filters or mechanisms to prevent AI use, or communicating about AI with parents. Thirty-nine percent of schools had implemented an AI policy for students, 18 percent had banned student use of AI outright, and 34 percent had installed filters or other mechanisms to prevent student AI use. Schools have addressed teacher use of AI far less frequently, with 7 percent of respondents indicating that their school had implemented an AI policy for teachers. As for communicating about AI with parents, half of schools (50 percent) had communicated with parents about AI in some way (figure 7).

Figure 7

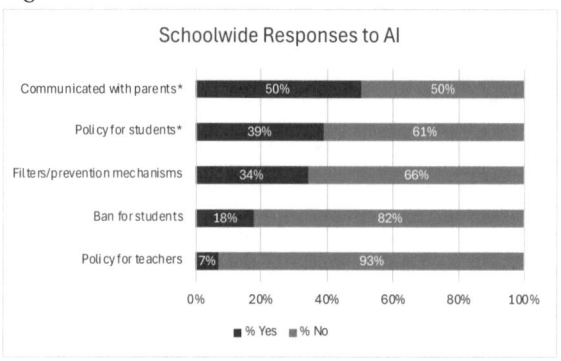

Schoolwide Responses to AI

Response	% Yes	% No
Communicated with parents*	50%	50%
Policy for students*	39%	61%
Filters/prevention mechanisms	34%	66%
Ban for students	18%	82%
Policy for teachers	7%	93%

Educator Perceptions Related to AI

The survey also asked about educators' perceptions of the potential benefits, risks, and applications of AI in Christian schools. Although the responses cannot be assumed predictive, educators' current perceptions can be helpful for considering possible future trends in AI adoption.

Overall, when asked how supportive they were of using AI in their school, 29 percent of survey respondents reported being supportive or very supportive, 40 percent were neutral, and 31 percent were not supportive. This suggests a significant undecided middle that has yet to determine their level of support for AI; this middle may change over time, depending on how AI uses develop or as their familiarity with AI grows. Interestingly, the percentage of educators who were unsupportive of AI use (31 percent) is close to the percentage of educators who responded no when asked whether AI can be used in ways that are compatible with biblical views. Although no cause or correlation is inferred, this suggests that theological questions concerning AI may be significant hurdles for schools looking to adopt AI, as it is likely that Christian educators will eschew teaching tools or methods they view as incompatible with biblical views.

Interestingly, there was a difference in educators' views of AI usage related to *themselves* versus their *students*. For example, when asked to gauge the likelihood of their recommending AI tools, educators indicated that they were more likely to recommend to colleagues than to students, at 45 percent and 32 percent, respectively (figure 8).

Figure 8

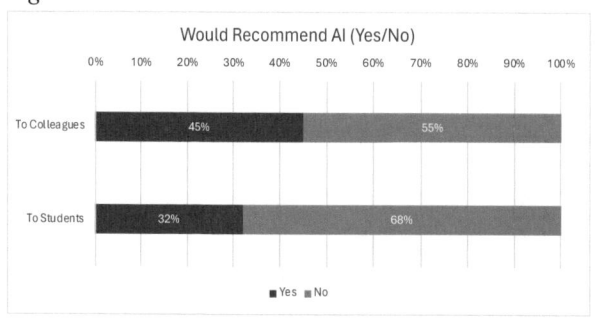

Would Recommend AI (Yes/No)

	Yes	No
To Colleagues	45%	55%
To Students	32%	68%

Two other data points may shed some light on this difference. When asked about specific benefits to teachers, most survey respondents agreed or strongly agreed that AI could help teachers save time and effort (87 percent), as well as develop more effective curriculum and lesson plans (60 percent) —reflecting a belief that AI has the capacity to make teaching easier and more effective. Conversely, educators expressed significant concern regarding student use of AI, most frequently identifying concerns related to ethics (i.e., cheating or other unethical behavior), the negative impact on student learning (i.e., hindering development of students' creative and critical-thinking skills), on safety (i.e., potential hacking or monitoring without consent), and on students' faith or values (figure 9).

Figure 9

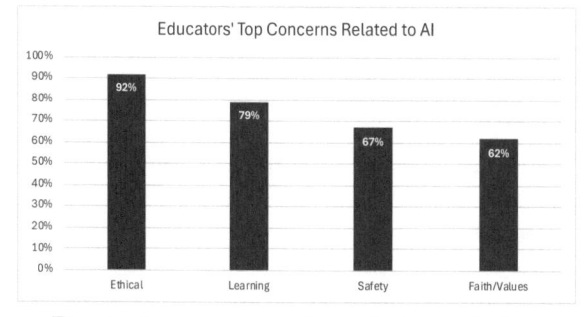

Educators' Top Concerns Related to AI

Ethical	Learning	Safety	Faith/Values
92%	79%	67%	62%

Despite these concerns, when asked to rank the aspects of schooling that they thought AI would have the greatest impact on in the future, a large majority (82 percent) of respondents chose teaching and learning as a top area. The next-highest area selected was administrative tasks, but at a distant second (48 percent), followed by student support services (27 percent) and student spiritual development (27 percent) (figure 10).

Figure 10

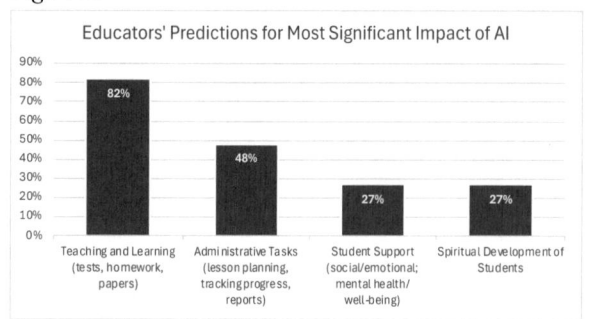

Educators' Predictions for Most Significant Impact of AI

- Teaching and Learning (tests, homework, papers): 82%
- Administrative Tasks (lesson planning, tracking progress, reports): 48%
- Student Support (social/emotional; mental health/well-being): 27%
- Spiritual Development of Students: 27%

When asked about specific areas of teaching and learning areas that they anticipate AI to have a significant impact on, the top areas chosen by educators were supporting students with special needs (89 percent), helping differentiate student learning (85 percent), and improving student engagement (75 percent) (figure 11).

Figure 11

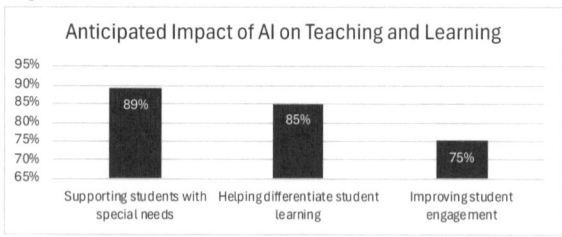

Anticipated Impact of AI on Teaching and Learning

- Supporting students with special needs: 89%
- Helping differentiate student learning: 85%
- Improving student engagement: 75%

Early Adopters of AI in Christian Schools

Taken together, the survey data suggest that the Christian school sector is in the early stages of AI adoption, with most educators reporting low levels of familiarity, usage, and confidence when it comes to AI technology. Similarly, most respondents (around two-thirds) indicated that their schools are not incorporating AI in teaching and learning. These levels contrast with educators' prediction that teaching and learning will be the area of schooling most impacted by AI in the future.

These data appear to concur with the assertion of many technologists and researchers[6] that generative AI is at the beginning of the technology S-curve (Foster 1986). This means that at this initial stage, *early adopters*—those who are the first to try out a new technology—are readily incorporating it into their practice, but the majority of potential users are not yet familiar or comfortable enough with the technology to adopt it. AI in education also appears to be in the second stage of the Gartner Hype Cycle, a five-stage model of the adoption of new technology. During this stage, known as the *Peak of Inflated Expectations*, early publicity results in stories of both success and failure, with most practitioners unsure of whether to adopt the new technology.

Regression analysis was used to identify the characteristics of educators and schools that correlate with higher levels of AI adoption.[7] No causal claim can be made, but this analysis yielded the following statistically significant correlations. First, there is a positive relationship between schools that have formally responded to AI and higher levels of educator familiarity. Second, there are generally more positive views of AI among administrators (versus teachers), urban school educators (versus suburban), and educators at missional (versus covenantal) schools.

School Responses and Educator Familiarity

Perhaps unsurprisingly, correlations were found between schoolwide responses to AI and educators' level of familiarity with AI, after controlling for a range of variables (figure 12). Analysis showed that educators who are familiar with AI have a greater likelihood of working in a school that uses AI in teaching and learning than educators who are not familiar with AI, by a large difference of about 37 percentage points ($p<0.01$). Similarly, educators who have more familiarity with AI are almost four times more likely to be in schools that have communicated about AI to their teachers and students than their counterparts who are not familiar with AI ($p<0.01$). Finally, schools that have communicated about AI to parents and students are also more likely to set policy around AI for their students, by about 47 percentage points ($p<0.01$)

---

6 See Grubbs (2023), Nasir (2023), and Scriven (2023).

7 On the graphs that follow in this section, we report statistical significance levels for each result where *** shows statistical significance at a 99 percent level of confidence ($p<0.01$) and ** represents a 95 percent level of confidence ($p<0.05$).

compared to schools that have not communicated about AI to their parents and students.

Figure 12

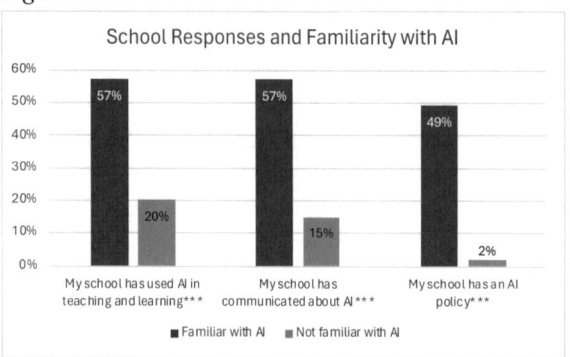

School Responses and Familiarity with AI

Category	Familiar with AI	Not familiar with AI
My school has used AI in teaching and learning***	57%	20%
My school has communicated about AI***	57%	15%
My school has an AI policy***	49%	2%

This study does not answer the question of which came first, a school's response to AI or educators' familiarity with AI. It also does not explain whether this relationship is reciprocal, with schoolwide responses to AI bolstering educator familiarity with AI, and vice versa. However, it does show that a positive relationship exists between the two—suggesting that schoolwide engagement with AI is connected to Christian school educators' familiarity with AI.

Administrators More Positive Than Teachers

Descriptive analysis of results found that administrators are more positive about AI than teachers in two areas: First, when it comes to agreeing that they are supportive of AI use (78 percent for administrators versus 63 percent for teachers); and second, that AI creates the opportunity for individualized feedback for students (75 percent for administrators versus 63 percent for teachers) (figure 13).

Philosophy and Research

Figure 13

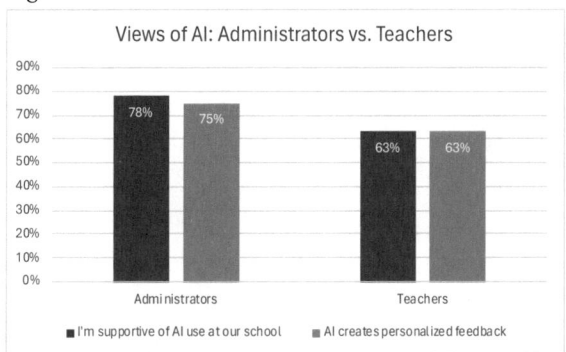

Views of AI: Administrators vs. Teachers

- Administrators: I'm supportive of AI use at our school: 78%; AI creates personalized feedback: 75%
- Teachers: I'm supportive of AI use at our school: 63%; AI creates personalized feedback: 63%

Using the study's analytical models, a statistically significant difference was also observed between administrators and teachers regarding their views of AI. These views tended to be more positive among administrators than teachers. Specifically, after controlling for variables using analytical models, administrators are more likely than teachers to agree that AI has more benefits than disadvantages by 9 percentage points ($p<0.01$). Teachers showed lower agreement (39 percent) than administrators (48 percent) as to whether AI should be incorporated in every classroom ($p<0.05$). Curiously, however, teachers were far more likely to agree than administrators that AI can help students learn better and faster, by a difference of 28 percentage points ($p<0.05$). This is the only area in which teachers were found to have a more positive view of AI than administrators (figure 14).

Figure 14

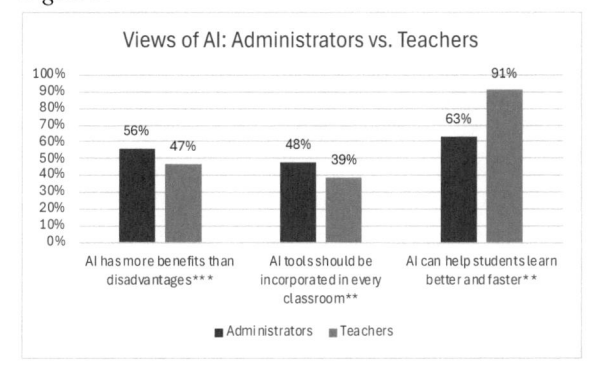

Views of AI: Administrators vs. Teachers

- AI has more benefits than disadvantages***: Administrators 56%, Teachers 47%
- AI tools should be incorporated in every classroom**: Administrators 48%, Teachers 39%
- AI can help students learn better and faster**: Administrators 63%, Teachers 91%

When these results are taken together, they suggest that administrators are more eager than teachers to see AI used in teaching and learning. This suggests a potential gap between administrator and teacher readiness for AI, with implications for leadership in Christian schools—namely that administrators seeking to adopt AI in their schools will need to address faculty reticence toward AI, perhaps through faculty trainings or other means that increase teacher awareness and comfort with AI.

Urban School Educators More Positive

On average, compared to suburban educators, educators in urban schools are more likely to agree, by about 15 percentage points (p<0.01), that AI has more benefits than disadvantages. Similarly, all else equal, there are more educators in suburban schools who agree that Christian school leaders should be concerned about the rise of AI technology for students than there are educators in urban schools, a difference of about 9 percentage points (p<0.05) (figure 15).

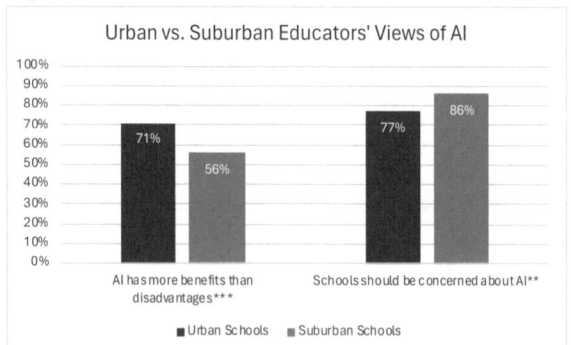

Figure 15

Urban vs. Suburban Educators' Views of AI

- AI has more benefits than disadvantages***: Urban Schools 71%, Suburban Schools 56%
- Schools should be concerned about AI**: Urban Schools 77%, Suburban Schools 86%

Interestingly, a correlation was found between educators' personal use of AI and their schools' urbanicity. Specifically, urban educators used AI with more frequency in personal settings than suburban educators, by a difference of 14 percentage points (p<0.01). Moreover, there is a large difference observed when comparing rural educators and suburban educators; rural educators are less likely to say that they use AI in their personal settings than suburban educators by about 20 percentage points (p<0.01) (figure 16).

Figure 16

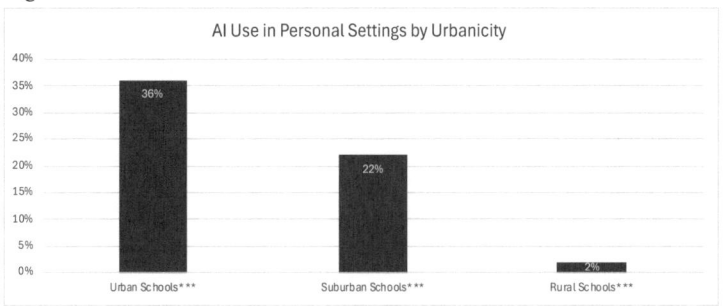

AI Use in Personal Settings by Urbanicity

- Urban Schools***: 36%
- Suburban Schools***: 22%
- Rural Schools***: 2%

Despite these findings, no correlation was observed between urbanicity and *professional* use of AI in schools. However, when it comes to *personal* use of AI, urban school educators are more likely to be early adopters, followed by suburban school educators.

Missional Schools More Positive

Finally, data analysis revealed significantly more positive views of AI among educators at missional schools versus covenantal schools. Specifically, educators at missional schools were more likely to affirm that technology is important for Christian schools (89 percent, versus 78 percent for covenantal), that AI has more benefits than drawbacks (73 percent, versus 56 percent), that AI can help students learn better and faster (65 percent, versus 51 percent), that AI can be used in ways that are compatible with biblical views (75 percent, versus 60 percent), and that AI can support students with special needs (95 percent, versus 86 percent) (figure 17). Lastly, on average, covenantal schools are four times more likely to ban the use of AI among students than missional schools ($p<0.01$).

Figure 17

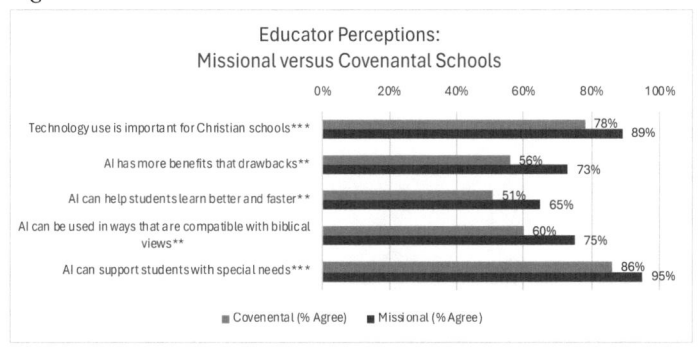

Educator Perceptions: Missional versus Covenantal Schools

Statement	Covenantal (% Agree)	Missional (% Agree)
Technology use is important for Christian schools***	78%	89%
AI has more benefits that drawbacks**	56%	73%
AI can help students learn better and faster**	51%	65%
AI can be used in ways that are compatible with biblical views**	60%	75%
AI can support students with special needs***	86%	95%

More research is needed to understand these observations related to more positive views of AI among missional school educators versus covenantal. However, one immediate implication is that positive use cases for AI in instruction may be more readily identifiable among missional schools.

Conclusion

This study yielded descriptive data on AI adoption among more than 700 Christian school leaders and teachers. The study found that on nearly all measures (schoolwide use of AI, as well as educator use and confidence level), less than a third of schools and educators could be considered as adopting AI. When we explore the factors that are correlated with early adoption of AI, more positive views of AI are found among leaders (versus teachers), greater usage among educators at schools that have taken formal steps to adopt or address AI, and correlations between demographic factors with more positive views of AI (i.e., greater urbanicity, as well as missional versus covenantal admissions policies).

This study provides a snapshot of AI implementation in Christian schools at a particular point in time. Future research will be needed to understand how schools respond to AI over the long term, particularly as educational use cases, educator familiarity with AI, and AI-related resources continue to grow. While insights from this study are useful to those seeking to understand early responses to AI in the Christian school sector, they are descriptive—*not* proscriptive. In other words, the study's data describe what *is* in Christian schools, not necessarily what *should be*. That latter question is best addressed by each Christian school community, relying on their unique missions—including their theological views and educational philosophies—to inform the question of whether and how to integrate AI technologies.

Part II:
Christian School Perspectives

The Head of School Perspective
Scott Harsh, *Greater Atlanta Christian School*

Greater Atlanta Christian School (GAC) is located in the metro-Atlanta area and serves close to 1,800 students in grades PreK–12 who come from more than eighty zip codes. During the past year, GAC has rolled out a new artificial-intelligence (AI) tutor in middle and high school grades. As opposed to other AI tutors in the marketplace, this AI tutor—called *TrekAI*—is unique in that it (1) is grounded in a Christian worldview, (2) draws from real curricula and classes in our school, and (3) operates on an inquiry or Socratic framework. This chapter aims to tell the story of AI implementation within our context, as well as share the learnings we have gathered along the way.

Building Up to AI

To tell the story of AI at GAC, we have to go back a few years. This is because GAC simply would not have been ready to launch TrekAI without years of previous foundational work. Our journey began in 2015, when our desire to broaden the GAC academic program led us to look for an online school with which to partner. We wanted to ensure that academic rigor, Christian perspective, and high engagement—three hallmarks of a GAC education—were reflected in the online program we chose. At that time, we simply could not find a program that met these criteria. So, we decided that if such a program did not yet exist, we would seek to launch our own.

We started the development process in what we would call the margins—in other words, the areas in which we needed the most help, and for which we surmised other schools would likewise need the most help. This meant we started with advanced placement (AP) and world language classes, because we were already offering more of those classes than most Christian schools at the time. Our online program, which we named Ethos, grew from that humble beginning of twenty courses to now offering over one hundred online courses in math, science, languages, social studies, the arts, Bible, English, and health and fitness. Today we have teachers both on our campus and around the world who teach in

Ethos, as well as close to seventy-five partner schools around the globe that use these courses. More importantly, we have external validation that our initial goals for online instruction—academic rigor, Christian perspective, and student engagement—have been achieved. Our students' pass rates are not only far above the national average but also nearly identical for both our AP courses taught through Ethos and those on campus. We also have many success stories from students who feel so engaged through Ethos that they ask the Ethos teachers to write college recommendations for them, because they feel their Ethos teachers are the ones who know them best.

Fast-forward to spring 2020 and the global pandemic. We didn't know at the time if the need for synchronous online instruction would last two months, ten months, or two years—but we knew GAC needed a tool that could provide engaged, online instruction. Moreover, we wanted to create a long-term strategy and not just meet immediate needs from the pandemic. GAC invested heavily in technology and teacher training, and from that season we launched what we call GAC Sync (for synchronous learning). Still in place today, GAC Sync covers all grades and classes from K–12 and enables students to participate live in their courses when they are not on campus. All students, in all grades, have a daily choice—they can be in our on-campus classrooms, or they can participate in class via GAC Sync. Most students choose on campus for the vast majority of the time, because they value engaging in person with their teachers and peers. But if a student is out sick, is traveling, or, for example, has several late nights with school activities and would benefit from some added rest and a day at home, Sync enables them to still engage fully in their education. Additionally, since each class is recorded, students can review their classes any number of times, as well as search within class recordings so they don't have to watch the entire class session. This provides all our students with an easy way to review course content on demand, whether they attend that day in person or participate remotely.

In short, as a result of launching Ethos and GAC Sync, we were able to build a data lake of all our curriculum and course content, composed of transcripts of all our own class sessions, class recordings, curricular materials, etc. In essence, our entire academic program had been digitized.

This provided the crucial foundational work and set the stage for what would come next.

Enter AI

In 2022, we began to see a new opportunity. With a fully digitized curriculum and access for students to be able to search content, we began to ask questions about how GAC could further personalize the learning experience for our students. We wanted to continue to move away from the industrial model of education—where every student spends the same amount of time in every course and every class has the same start and end time, both daily and throughout the year. We began to hear about generative AI and its emerging applications in education, as well as that a majority of students—upward of 90 percent—report using ChatGPT and social media outlets in their studies (Rispens 2023). We recognized an opportunity with AI to further propel our long-term strategy toward personalized learning. And just as we did with online education, we began asking if we could launch our own platform—one that, again, met our own standards of academic rigor, Christian perspective, and high engagement. We realized that if we could give an AI tutor rules, a way of thinking, and a way of teaching through prompt engineering —and then layer it on top of our curriculum—we would have a powerful new tool to support our students' learning. In spring 2023, we partnered with a group of software developers to build the platform. We began working with teachers to answer questions like the following: How do we create an AI tutor in a way that would deeply engage students (i.e., through inquiry and the Socratic method) rather than simply spitting out answers, and how could we ensure that our Christian worldview is built right into the AI tutor itself?

Through this collaborative effort, we developed TrekAI over spring and summer 2023. Beginning in August 2023, we then piloted TrekAI with a small number of our teachers and students. As of spring 2024, all our students in middle and high school have access to TrekAI, and we are piloting it with an additional twelve Christian schools. TrekAI helps students in real time, whether by generating practice questions for an upcoming test or running a term paper draft through the teacher's rubric to get feedback and make improvements before turning it in. GAC now has a personalized tutor that can be helpful to students in their current coursework—and that personalized tutor is available twenty-four hours per day, seven days a week. Perhaps because of this level of availability, research has shown that students prefer an AI tutor to a live tutor (*The Week* 2023) because unlike a live tutor, TrekAI fits anywhere into students' schedules, whether between school and sports practice, or in the car on the ride home, or late at night when teachers aren't available via email. That real-time tutor comes alongside students, not to replace teachers, but to enhance the learning experience and to drive inquiry and mastery.

The Student Journey

Research has demonstrated the positive impact of an AI tutor on student learning (*The Week* 2023). We have seen this with our own students at GAC. In late fall 2023, our internal study found that 93 percent of students using TrekAI said it helped improve their grades, and we found that 14 percent of positive change in student grades was driven by TrekAI usage.

In terms of adoption, there has been significant interest and excitement among the student body (though, of course, just like our faculty, some students are early adopters and some are more hesitant to try new technology). We have seen some variability in terms of grade levels: Our middle school students and younger high school students are more prone to higher levels of chat usage, perhaps because juniors and seniors are more comfortable with the methods they have honed throughout their formative years for studying and writing. We have also noted that students use TrekAI most frequently in English and math classes, though the tool is available and used across all subjects. This may be because English teachers have been significant promoters of TrekAI as they see the way that the tool can help students improve their work. And for math, students may more easily see the opportunity for AI to help them understand a challenging concept or generate practice problems.

By tracking usage of TrekAI across the academic year, we recognized a significant spike in use in the two weeks leading up to finals. One surprising use of TrekAI is how students will leverage it in study group settings. Just before finals in fall 2023, our high school principal observed a group of students gathering around one student's laptop in the student commons just before they were about to head into a final exam. They were using TrekAI to generate practice questions—much as they would engage with a teacher in a pre-exam review, just to ensure they were ready for the test—and answering the questions together. This shows that students see TrekAI as a tool they can trust.

It's important to note that we haven't just put TrekAI in our students' hands and walked away. Rather, we scaffold its usage with our students. At the beginning of each semester, our dean for technology and innovation visits each class to introduce TrekAI, talk about ideal uses, and answer student questions. We also work with older students to consider the bigger questions around AI. For example, our senior capstone Bible course engages students in discussion around a number of contemporary issues, including AI, and how to think about those issues from a Christian perspective. And we have been intentional about engaging students' parents as well. Throughout the year, our Parent Speaker Series features authors and speakers on parenting and student issues. One of the sessions focused on AI and included a broad overview of how we think about AI, what students are currently doing with AI, what TrekAI is, and what it means for students.

The Teacher Journey

In addition to the AI tutor for students, we simultaneously built a whole suite of tools in TrekAI for teachers. These tools enable feedback loops that are tremendously beneficial for teaching and learning. For example, TrekAI enables teachers to track the kinds of questions students are asking when they're not in their classes, and teachers can adjust instruction accordingly. Teachers can also load their course rubrics into TrekAI so students can assess their own work without just relying on teachers for feedback on drafts; teachers can be assured the AI tutor will provide the same kind of feedback that they themselves would give. Teachers can also use TrekAI to generate better questions for tests and assignments to improve their teaching.

Even though this suite of tools exists, we knew we had to scaffold the process of integrating TrekAI for teachers. As with any new technology, there will always be an adoption curve—starting with early adopters, who then become influencers to a second group who sees what's happening and wants to be a part, to another group who is toward the tail end of the curve and slower to adopt. Because of the forward-thinking culture we have built at GAC, our teachers in general lean more toward the first half of the curve, but we certainly have teachers who fall into all groups. Thus we started by piloting TrekAI for a semester in a few select classes, versus launching across the entire school at once. We wanted to have early success on which we could then build. Our pilot involved six teachers who were eager because they saw the potential of TrekAI and found the opportunity to help us design an AI tutor appealing. With our launch of Ethos, GAC Sync, and now TrekAI, we have also staffed up to support teachers. We have a dean of innovation and technology, an Ethos academic dean, instructional lead teachers, and others who are coming alongside teachers to provide professional development as well. Finally, we have built-in feedback loops where teachers can share what works and what doesn't, tips to improve the tool, and ways we can provide better training and support for teachers.

When it comes to the teacher journey, it's important to note that the launch of TrekAI followed on the heels of years of professional development in using digital resources in teaching and learning. Our view of AI at GAC is shaped by how we think about teaching and learning overall: We look to the example of the master teacher Himself, Jesus. Thus, our goals are always to create the very best learning environment for our students, to be thoughtful together as a community of educators, to use research to inform how we teach, and to find great partners who can join us to help us educate with excellence.

Aligning to Our Mission

When it comes to AI, it is non-negotiable that Christian schools consider how it aligns with their Christian worldview and their mission as a school. As with any resource we'd give to students, the source of Truth has to be firmly in place. This means that if we simply adopt any tool that's in the secular marketplace, it certainly could be helpful to our students—but it also could be really harmful because of the content from which it pulls. If an AI tutor pulls from the internet as a whole, just like Google, that is the scope of content that can end up in students' hands. With GAC's TrekAI, the tutor pulls from our teachers' content first; if it can't find the right content, it will go beyond to the internet, but we have put rules and guidelines in place to ensure that the responses are still aligned with our Christian perspective. For example, there are certain issues and questions that will automatically elicit a response from TrekAI that the student should seek out the help of a trusted adult. In this way, we ensure that the AI tool our students use is aligned with our Christian perspective and mission.

Again, aligning with our mission is true of everything we do in teaching—and not just in Bible classes, but also how we teach science, math, English, and every subject. It shapes who we hire, the ways we coach, how we manage our classrooms, and everything in between. It includes books, curricula, and other materials that we select for our academic program. Just as we think about biblical alignment in every other aspect of the GAC student experience, we ought to be thinking about mission alignment when we consider the AI tools and other technology that we put into the hands of our students.

Our Learning for Schools

As I've shared in this chapter, it's been a long and extensive journey for GAC to get to this point with AI. We have talked with many schools along the way, and we've found that most Christian school leaders want to be proactive and look for positive solutions to the AI question. Their most common concern at the start is how to put up guardrails to ensure that students aren't taking shortcuts in the learning process, shortcuts that ultimately would be harmful to their learning (and to them as individuals). In response, we counsel leaders to do three things when it comes to AI: first, take a proactive approach. Second, integrate the same faith perspective that would be required in any of your programs. And third, consider strategic, long-term goals—not just immediate wins.

It's this long-term strategy that is essential for the future. This strategy gives us both a sense of direction and a momentum to keep moving in that direction. This is crucial because we don't know the next technological innovation that will come along. But if we are constantly engaged in scanning the horizon, experimenting, piloting, and evaluating, we can move forward even if there are new technologies we decide not to adopt or pivots we need to make when it comes to a specific technology. At GAC, our AI story is not really about AI per se. It's about continuing to build a culture where we think about the future of learning and where we do not stay stuck in our current iteration of schooling—because we know there's a future coming that will look different than today. Of course, this has real implications for everything from staffing to scheduling decisions. But our overall stance is that we need to be nimble in order to be ready for the future and to prepare our students for their own future.

Finally, we are convinced that Christian schools need to partner with one another to create a stronger future for all Christian schools. We simply cannot address individually the technological opportunities and challenges that are rapidly coming our way. This doesn't mean that all Christian schools respond to AI and new technologies in the same way. But because of our common mission, we need to think about our responses in ways that are different from other educational sectors—and we need each other to do that successfully.

Looking to the Future

Personalization is happening in all areas of our lives—and education is next. If we stop to think about it, our current model of education is a newer model. For most of recorded human history, education happened by apprenticeship of some sort—with a master teacher engaging and guiding a single student or a very small group of students at most. The problem with this historical approach to education—and what eventually led to the industrialized model we have today—is that it wasn't scalable. But now, with generative AI learning, we are on the cusp of being able to return to that personalized level of learning that apprenticeships once offered.

At GAC, we do not foresee an entirely digital future for learning. We still want in-person, face-to-face engagement with and between teachers and students, as well as students interacting with one another. Life-on-life engagement is key to both deep learning and authentic discipleship, both of which are central to Christian education. Rather than replacing teachers, we have an opportunity to enable teachers to do more of what we've always wanted them to do—to come alongside students, to mentor and guide them, and to invest in their lives. This becomes much more possible with the help of digital tools, because it is no longer incumbent upon the teacher to provide all the content, all the time, at the same exact pace for all students. Digital tools open new possibilities for what the design of classes and schools will look like. It will create new possibilities for our students, as their learning becomes deeper, more personalized, and more engaging. We see opportunities for our teachers to become the facilitators and guides that our students need, in a fuller way. And it will allow schools to consider how they can go deeper and further in fulfilling their missions, both now and into the future.

Christian School Perspectives

The Teacher Perspective
Paul Matthews, *MyTeacherAide*

There are decades where nothing happens, and there are weeks where decades happen.[1]

My colleague furrowed his brow as he watched ChatGPT string out lines of text on my screen. After a few moments of silence, he put his head in his hands. "This changes everything," he sighed.

I could tell he met the change with fatigue and hesitation. He, like many educators, wished for a simpler time—a time when innovation wasn't progressing at breakneck speed. We are truly living in the weeks where decades happen, and many teachers wish it were not so.

Nostalgia for simpler times is a natural response to rapid change. Yet, as Christians, the reality is that if God wanted us to live in a different age, that's where He would have put us. But He didn't. He put us here amid the most rapid revolution the world has ever known. In His providence, He has entrusted us to wisely steward this generation of students through this generation of challenges.

Note that our task is not to batten down the hatches and weather the storm. It's not merely to limit the damage caused by new technology. Our task is to use this new technology in such a way that glorifies God, loves others, avoids the pitfalls, and embraces the benefits. The call on Christian educators is not merely to survive, but to lead.

In this chapter, I will focus on how teachers can lead their students and themselves through the disruption of artificial intelligence (AI).[2] I will do this using the LEAD framework:
- **L**iving under lordship
- **E**ngaging ethically
- **A**dapting appropriately
- **D**iscussing discerningly

---

1 While this quote is often attributed to Vladamir Lenin, it is not found in any of his written or recorded work.

2 In speaking of AI, I am referring to generative AI tools such as ChatGPT, Bard, Midjourney, and other large language model tools.

After exploring the LEAD framework, I will suggest practical and redemptive uses of AI in the classroom. This will include some basic AI skills such as how to prompt a large language model (LLM) like ChatGPT, and how to create learning activities, rubrics, assessments, and more.

It's my earnest hope that, after you have read this chapter, you will be theologically and practically equipped to LEAD yourself and your students through these times of rapid change.

Living Under Lordship

As Christian educators, we begin our response to AI with the most basic of Christian creeds: Christ is Lord. This profession bears witness to the truth that there is no authority beyond Christ. Not only did Jesus become a man, live a sinless life, and die in our place, He also ascended "into heaven and is at the right hand of God, with angels, authorities, and powers having been subjected to Him" (1 Peter 3:22). As He rules from His throne, He has a rightful claim over all things (Kuyper, in Bratt 1998), including technology. As we navigate our way through emerging technologies, we must live, work, and walk under the lordship of Christ. His lordship is our north star, our founding principle. Without it, we will be prone to drift into fear on one hand, or idolatry on the other. Living under lordship helps us confront technology in several important ways.

Freedom from Fear

Rapid technological change can give us a profound sense of fear. We have no idea what lies ahead, and we feel ill-equipped for what we may encounter. This fear is common among Christians, with author Tony Reinke (2022) arguing, "In the church, fear is winning out over faith when it comes to technology" (23). Fear of the unknown is a natural instinct that we must confront with supernatural truth.

As Christians, we know that even when earth seems to be in a state of flux, the courts of heaven remain unchanged. Indeed, our Lord "is the same yesterday and today and forever" (Hebrews 13:8). AI did not take Christ by surprise, and no technological disruption will disrupt His love, care, and provision for His people. Indeed, we must remember that every believer has God's Spirit, which is "a spirit not of fear but of power and love and self-control" (2 Timothy 1:7). Living under the lordship of Christ will free us from the fear of change and the unknown.

Escape from Idolatry

While some people fear rapid change, others swerve into the opposite ditch. Perhaps one of the besetting sins of our age is an idolatry of technology. Everyone has a worldview, whether expressed or implied. Everyone has answers to the questions: "What's gone wrong, and how do we fix it?" (Walsh and Middleton 1984). For many, the big problem with our world is not moral but technological. They suppose that the needs we face on a daily basis, whether hunger, disease, or disaster, will eventually be put out of commission when our technology becomes advanced enough.

While faith in technology bears little resemblance to bowing to an Asherah pole, modern technophiles are every bit the idolaters as the ancient Canaanites; they are still prone to worship and serve created things "rather than the Creator" (Romans 1:25). Modern technology produces great tools but terrible saviors. If the twentieth century has taught us anything, it is that prophets of the technological utopia radically overpromise and underdeliver. Living under the lordship of Christ will free us from the sin and continual disappointment of idolizing technology.

Get the Best out of Technology

Having avoided the opposite errors of fear and idolatry, living under the lordship of Christ allows us to get the best out of technology. Tony Reinke (2022) describes technology as taking the patterns and elements of our created world to amplify our abilities, allowing us to do more faster and better than we could in our own strength. One of the great questions that technology poses, given that it allows us to do more and do it faster, is, What shall we use it for? Reinke goes on, "The true challenge … is not in determining which technologies should be made possible but in determining how those new possibilities are wielded. Thus, Scripture puts the emphasis not on the technology, but on how those innovations are used" (70).

As Christians who have the mind (Philippians 2:5) and the Spirit (Ephesians 1:13) of Christ, we can use these technologies in a way that acknowledges the lordship of Christ and furthers His kingdom. Christ came to feed the hungry, and with technology, we have reduced the global undernourishment rate dramatically in the last sixty years (FAO 2010). Christ came to heal the sick, and over the last decades, infant mortality, deaths in childbirth, and deaths from cancer, tuberculosis, and malaria have all fallen dramatically (Bailey and Tupy 2020). This is not to claim that technology replaces the work of Christ, but that Christians, with the mind and Spirit of Christ, can continue this work, aided by technology.

Living under lordship allows us to flee from fear, escape idolatry, and get the best out of technology. But using technology well isn't as simple as using it for noble purposes. So we not only ask what to do with technology but also what technology does with us.

Engaging Ethically

As we seek to LEAD ourselves and our students into the AI world, we must engage with emerging technologies ethically. Firstly, this involves acknowledging the formational power within new technology and redoubling our enthusiasm for being shaped into the image of Christ (Romans 8:29) and not conformed to the pattern of this world (Romans 12:2). Secondly, it involves emphasizing godly character and fleeing from sin when using this technology.

Central to our ethical use of AI and emerging technology, we must understand how it is prone to shape us. Our world is full of influences that shape who we are, what we love, and how we act. Ideas, people, environments, and technologies have a formative effect on us. It is with this in mind that the apostle Paul wrote, "Do not be conformed to this world, but be transformed by the renewal of your mind" (Romans 12:2).

Down in the DNA of every new technology, including the various manifestations of AI, there is a story being told about the world (Schuurman 2017, 4–11). It's this story, when imbibed and accepted, that can change us, often dramatically. Neil Postman, a cultural critic and technology commentator, argued, "Embedded in every technology there is a powerful idea, sometimes two or three powerful ideas" (Postman 1995). Our ethical beliefs and moral actions are shaped by the "ideas" embedded within the technology we use. This sentiment is captured in the idea that "we shape our tools, and then our tools shape us." The "stories" within the technology may have been deliberately constructed by the corporations who built them, or they may be an unintended by-product. Either way, these ideas are compelling and formative. Let us briefly examine some of the stories contained within AI tools that have become ubiquitous.

Snapchat

In April 2023, Snapchat launched an AI chatbot within its popular app. With no warning, training, or prior consideration, 750 million users had access to an AI chatbot at their fingertips. Early criticism of the feature centered on inappropriate responses given by the chatbot. There were screenshots being shared of the chatbot telling underage partygoers how to mask the smell of alcohol and marijuana (Fowler 2023) or engage in underage sex and lie to their parents about it (Smith 2023).

While these reports are concerning, little was said about the deeper story within an AI chatbot used by hundreds of millions of teens. If I had to guess, the following ideas are contained within tools like this:

- Conversations should be about the topics I want to talk about, and they should last as long as I want them to.
- A good conversation is one where I have my emotional and intellectual needs met in a way that feels right to me. A bad conversation is one where my conversational partner doesn't tell me what I want to hear or engage with me in a way that feels good.

While accessing age-inappropriate information is concerning, more concerning still is that this technology could shape a student's entire understanding of interpersonal relationships. The ideas within this technology could transform every relationship a student has for the worse.

ChatGPT

In November 2022, Open AI launched ChatGPT. For many, it was their first use of an AI built from an LLM. It left users in awe as it produced novel, engaging, and seemingly intelligent content. As with Snapchat's My AI, much of the critique has revolved around incorrect output (Bordoloi 2023). But on a deeper level than the accuracy of output, what are the stories and ideas embedded within a technology like this?

Here are a few of my best guesses:
- It would be a waste of my time learning to do any task that an AI can complete to a higher standard and in less time.
- I don't need to wrestle with deep questions because I can ask an AI that will give me an instant answer to any question I may have.
- I don't need to stare at a blank page waiting for inspiration. I can simply get ChatGPT to write a full first draft of my work, and then I can curate the output.

While the accuracy of information is important, more important is a student's understanding of learning, creativity, and the value of knowledge, all of which are impacted by the story within an LLM AI like ChatGPT.

Ethical Engagement

How do we engage with these tools ethically? How can we be sure that we aren't being unwittingly formed by the powerful ideas embedded within these technologies?

Firstly, the simple activity of discerning the stories or ideas within the new technology is a confident step in the right direction. Bringing these stories to light removes one of the most formative aspects of technology: our ignorance of its shaping power. Once brought out into the open, we can have discussions (more on this later) in community about how this formation aligns with God's vision for our lives and what steps we can take to ensure we are being transformed by the renewing of our minds, not being conformed to the pattern of this world.

Secondly, we must navigate new technologies with ancient morality. More than ever, we need integrity, wisdom, self-control, and love. We must encourage ourselves and our students to "turn away from evil and do good" (Psalm 34:14). While this kind of exhortation has always been a part of Christian education, we must proclaim it with renewed vigor. The temptations of our age are not new, but the frequency and intensity of the temptations are. Put simply, it's never been this easy to sin.

Take cheating on homework, for example. While students have been cheating on their homework as long as there has been homework, it's easier now than it's ever been. In the past, cheating may have involved a parent, friend, or tutor completing the work, or finding a relevant book and copying a passage or stealing an idea. While it was possible to cheat, it wasn't necessarily easy. Now, every student with internet access can simply copy and paste a question into ChatGPT and have an answer in seconds. It's the same temptation, but far more accessible. Because there has never been an easier time to cheat, there has never been a more important time for integrity.

The same goes for interpersonal relationships. Selfishness is a temptation everyone faces. However, in the age of plutonic and romantic AI chatbots, the idea that relationships are meant to satisfy our own needs will become increasingly common. More than ever, we must remind ourselves and our students that it is "more blessed to give than to receive" (Acts 20:35) and that we must consider not only our own needs, but also the needs of others (Philippians 2:4).

Adapting Appropriately

As we live under the lordship of Christ and engage with AI ethically, we must then consider how we can adapt appropriately. Let me give you the bottom line up front: The world we are teaching in now is radically different than it was three years ago. We are teaching in a new world, an AI world. We must adapt. Consider the following line from *The Lord of the Rings: The Fellowship of the Ring*: "The world has changed. I see it in the water. I feel it in the earth. I smell it in the air. Much that once was is lost" (Tolkien 1954). The change wrought by AI isn't limited to the fact that we have a few more tools available. No, artificial intelligence—much like the change described by Tolkien—has changed everything.

Neil Postman argued that technological change is not additive but ecological. An example of additive change is adding a book to a bookshelf. After the new volume has been added, the shelf is exactly as it was before but with one extra book. That's not how technology changes the world. After the printing press, Europe was not the same old Europe but with more books. It was a whole new Europe. The West, in the clutches of social media, is not the same as it used to be, just with more apps. It became a whole new society. New technology changes the whole environment; it does not add something—it changes everything (Postman 1998).

New technology creates a new world. The more powerful the technology, the grander the scale of change. The ecological change brings advantages and trade-offs, some of which are immediately apparent, many of which must be carefully discerned. While many argue the merit of the advantages or the seriousness of the trade-offs, there can be no argument on one point: AI has caused a seismic change in our society.

Here is where things get serious for Christian teachers: We are not educating in the same world we were three years ago. You may drive the same car to work, and your school grounds may not have changed, but you are teaching in a different world. The ecological change wrought by AI is massive; we are only just starting to see the disruption unfold. We need not fear these changes. As mentioned previously, fear is not befitting the call of the Christian, and it can be banished as we live under the lordship of Christ. We must, however, adapt appropriately.

The first step toward adaptation is acknowledging a change has taken place. Here are just some of the changes we see in the AI world:

- Students can complete assignments with a fraction of the time and effort using AI.
- Traditional methods of measuring academic integrity are ineffective—every output from an LLM AI is unique and cannot be measured against a database for similarity.
- Students—many of whom feel the changes caused by AI more keenly than their teachers—are scared of graduating into a world where machines can perform every task to a higher standard and for less money (Hamilton et al. 2023).
- Teachers have the ability to create tailored resources for their students in a fraction of the time it used to take, resources that allow for more personalized learning.
- Every student with internet access can be trained to use AI as a tutor. Immediate, tailored feedback is now no longer only for those with the financial means to hire a tutor.
- Teachers can create high-quality lesson plans, rubrics, and assessments more quickly than ever before.
- Our frequent AI use is giving large tech corporations wholesale access to more of our data than ever before.

Some of these changes are good. Some of these are bad. We may think some are good and they turn out to be bad, and vice versa. But one thing is for certain: They are all changes that we need to navigate together.

Discussing Discerningly

The final step of the LEAD framework is discerning discussions. It is these discussions that allow classrooms and school communities to manage change during the AI revolution. The adaptations required by the ecological change of AI will be significant. Even if schools can adapt appropriately, it won't be easy for the school community. When poorly managed, attempts at organizational change can result in rumors, frustration, resistance, and a failure to achieve meaningful change (Lewis 2019). Research shows that between 50 and 70 percent of planned change efforts fail (Mansaray 2019, 18–31). While there are many different frameworks for managing change in an organization, the lowest common denominator is they all include communication with stakeholders.

However, for a Christian school and for Christian teachers, communication itself isn't enough. It's not enough that discussions are taking place—they must be *discerning* discussions. There is a type of conversation that actually makes things worse. As mentioned earlier, many meet this AI world with considerable fear. Others are prone to idolize the technology. Some resent tech companies for creating the tech, students for using the tech, and schools for adapting to the tech. As we seek to adapt appropriately, we must manage this not only with discussions but also with discerning discussions. Discerning discussions:

- keep the lordship of Christ central;
- acknowledge the difficulty of change;
- honor the efforts of school leaders, teachers, students, and parents;
- encourage all to live in fellowship by faith, not fractured by fear;
- seek to bring the Scriptures to bear on our thoughts, words, and circumstances;
- encourage and build up one another;
- spur one another on toward love and good deeds; and
- do not slander others.

It would be easy for school leaders to imagine that change must be managed between school leadership and teaching staff. While these are crucial audiences involved in discerning discussions, students and parents also need to be involved. Below is a list of questions I have been asked by students, teachers, and parents during my consulting and teaching. They give an idea of the scope of the discussions we must be having as Christian schools.

Students
- Will there be any jobs left for me by the time I graduate? What does the future look like?
- Why do I need to write/spell/research/solve equations when AI can do it better and faster?
- When is using AI cheating, and when is it useful?
- I am trying to not cheat with AI, but I know other students who are, and they're getting away with it.
- How can I use AI to improve my learning?
- Why bother learning when we will soon have the technology to implant knowledge directly into our brains?

Teachers
- How can AI help me reduce my workload?
- If AI does reduce my workload, will the school leadership simply expect me to take on more work?
- Is it ethically right for me to create resources with AI if I've instructed my students not to use it?
- How can I tell when my students are being academically dishonest by using AI inappropriately?
- How much AI use is appropriate for which task?
- Do I have to go back to pen and paper, in-class, exam-style assessments to prevent cheating with AI?

Parents
- How do I know if my son or daughter is using AI to complete his or her work?
- My child is anxious about the future. How can I counsel him or her well during this time?

- I don't think the school is making wise decisions concerning AI. Who can I discuss this with?
- Why is my son or daughter still learning to write? All he or she should be learning is to manage AI. This is what the future of work looks like.
- I fear my child is too reliant on technology and isn't being educated in the basics of reading, writing, and arithmetic.

While discussions like this can be difficult, it's freeing to know we don't always need to have the "right" answers. For some questions, we will be able to give a clear, well-informed answer. For other questions, such as the future of work, we may need to make an educated guess, acknowledge our inability to tell the future, and rejoice that there is one in heaven who has gone before us and will care for His children no matter what the future looks like (1 Peter 5:7).

A commitment to discerning discussions acknowledges that navigating life as a Christian isn't something we do on our own. It's something we do together. We must "one another" our way through this. Ultimately, open communication and discerning discussions within our school communities allow us to achieve the first three objectives of the LEAD framework: living under the lordship of Christ, fleeing fear, and avoiding idolatry; engaging ethically with technology, avoiding unconscious formation and resisting temptation; and adapting appropriately, leveraging the benefits and avoiding the pitfalls of new technology. In short, navigating the AI world well is a whole-community project. And, as with any community project, we must keep the lines of communication open and discuss discerningly.

Practical Ways to LEAD

As teachers, leaders, and Christian school communities, we must commit to wisely navigating the rapid change caused by AI. Artificial intelligence isn't going anywhere, and it's not the sort of thing that we will navigate well by accident. Rather than ignoring or resenting change, we can commit to LEAD well in our classrooms and schools. But as the old saying goes, "You can't learn to ride a bike at a seminar." While framing our use of and adaption to AI is helpful, using AI is vital to helping our communities navigate the problems and possibilities of these technologies.

I will conclude this chapter by offering some simple frameworks and activities that you can use as you begin to use AI tools.

Power Up Your Prompts: The RTF Framework

There is an old saying in the AI community: "Garbage in, garbage out." Most people are frustrated by the bland and boring output AI gives them; the truth is, however, that they are using bland and boring prompts. When learning to use AI, learning to prompt is a great place to start. While there are many prompting frameworks, the one I use most is the RTF framework:

- **R**ole. Give the AI a role; this will usually start with "Act as a …" or "You are a …"
- **T**ask. Give the AI the task you want completed. It will be something like "Turn these dot points into full sentences," "Rewrite this text into simpler language," or "Write me a summary of the second chapter of *To Kill a Mockingbird*."
- **F**ormat. Be specific with the kind of output you want. Do you want it in paragraphs, in dot points, in a grid or a table, or at a specific word count or reading level? The more specific you can be, the better the output.

Here is an example of a prompt using the RTF framework: "(ROLE) Act as a Year 10 English teacher. (TASK) Write a summary of Chapter 2 of *To Kill a Mockingbird* by Harper Lee. (FORMAT) Present it to me in five paragraphs of 250 words each, with dot-point summaries after each paragraph."

Specific Ways to Use Prompts

As an educator, you can tailor your prompts for specific classroom applications and learning objectives. Some examples are the following:

- **Flipped Classroom.** Before starting a new unit, it's a great idea to have students do some prereading on the topic. This will help them develop a schema where they can place the information they learn during the unit. I give my students the following prompt: "Act as a [year/subject] teacher. Give me five key pieces of information about [subject/topic/person]. Display each piece of information in a paragraph of 150 words at a [year] reading level."

- **Examining Contested Ideas.** One of the most fascinating things about a topic of study is the way that it is disputed or contested among different groups. When studying a new topic, ask students to find different perspectives on the topic. I give my students the following prompt: "Act as a [year/subject] teacher. I am studying [topic/person/place]. Explain the different points of view or schools of thought on [topic/person/place]. Present your information at a [year] reading level."
- **Creating Tailored Questions.** As educators, we know that learning is not just about what you put into the student's head but also what you draw out. Retrieval practice has a strong evidence base and can greatly improve learning outcomes. The problem is that tests and quizzes are time-consuming to create. Try using the following prompt for creating simple, low-stakes quizzes/questions for your class: "Act as a [year/subject] teacher. I will paste in an article, and I want you to create a list of questions based on the five Es framework (Engage, Explore, Explain, Elaborate, and Evaluate). Create two questions for each level of the framework. Ensure that the questions are suitable for a [year] student."
- **Text Differentiation.** The achievement gap in our classrooms has never been bigger. It's vital to ensure that students have access to the learning materials, and the first step in this process is ensuring they are able to read your text. Text differentiation is traditionally time-consuming and difficult. With AI, it's easier than ever to ensure that your students have learning materials that meet them where they're at. Along these lines, I give my students the following prompt: "Act as an expert educator who has a deep understanding of [content/subject area]. Simplify the text with these changes: Use shorter sentences, use easier words, and avoid idioms for clearer language suitable for English learners. Don't add new information unless it's necessary for understanding. The revised text should be roughly the same length as the original."

Iteration Is Key

The reason many educators are frustrated with AI is because they use it as a "guess-what's-in-my-head" machine. AI is a great tool but a terrible mind reader. In your practice, you'll find that creating prompts is a great place to start, but iteration is key. Iteration involves continuing the conversation with the AI, giving it feedback, and asking it to reshape or build on the output.

You will often find yourself saying things like the following:
- Rewrite this in less-formal language.
- Rewrite in fewer words.
- You missed one part of my prompt; don't forget to _____.
- Rewrite the output; focus less on _____ and more on _____.
- Please clarify the meaning of _____.

Don't expect the AI to come up with the perfect solution right away. Iteration is key to getting great output from AI.

Having examined the basics of prompting and explored some use cases, it's now time for you to continue your practice with new use cases. Perhaps you want to explore using AI to write rubrics, draft lesson plans, or create mock work samples to critique with a class. Use the RTF framework, draft and develop your prompts, and practice your iteration. Finally, remember that you will rarely take the output of an AI and use it with your class immediately. More often than not, you will need to edit the output to fit within your context. You are the professional; you know your subject, students, and school context.

As Christian schools seek to LEAD in the AI world, we must do so with discernment. This doesn't involve just getting all the right answers—it must involve asking ourselves the right questions: How has our world changed, and how can we adapt appropriately? Further, schools are communities. It is not up to one leader or a small working group to ask and answer these questions. It is a process for the whole community. As you consider how to use AI in your classroom and in your school in wise ways, may you join with fellow Christian educators to seek discernment and the wisdom that comes from above (James 3:17).

The Student Perspective
Lynn E. Swaner, *Cardus*, and
Derek Wilson, *Greater Atlanta Christian School*

The adoption of new instructional technology is dependent upon how, and to what degree, educators incorporate that technology in their teaching strategies. At the same time, adoption of instructional technology also involves students—in terms of not only how they engage with the technology but also how it shapes their learning. In other words, adoption of a new instructional technology, like AI, is a two-way street. As such, it is important to examine and understand students' experiences of engaging with AI in the classroom.

To this end, a virtual focus group was conducted with students at Greater Atlanta Christian School (GAC) in Norcross, Georgia, in March 2024. GAC students were chosen intentionally for the focus group—as opposed to a cross section of students from different schools—because GAC is in the process of adopting AI in mission-aligned, thoughtful, and proactive ways. Given the variability of AI adoption across Christian schools, the goal of this focus group was to explore students' experiences at a school that is not only further down the track of AI adoption but also intentional in adopting AI in mission-aligned ways.

Eight students participated in the focus group, which was cofacilitated by an external researcher and GAC's dean of technology and innovation. All students in the group were either juniors or seniors, with five female and three male students. Guided by a set of questions, participants were asked to speak about their experiences with the school's internal AI tool (TrekAI) as well as other tools like ChatGPT. This chapter shares students' responses regarding (1) their use of AI in school, (2) beneficial ways their teachers have used AI, (3) their impressions of the AI rollout at their school, (4) their concerns about AI, and (5) their impressions of how AI relates to their Bible learning and faith formation.

Throughout this chapter, we present students' responses with minimal framing or interpretation, so as to allow students' voices to be "heard" directly by the reader. While we do not provide identifying student information to preserve participant anonymity, quotes in each section are presented in bulleted paragraph form, which indicates a response from a unique student.

Student Use of AI

We first asked how often students used AI tools and for what tasks they used them. The frequency of student usage ranged from twice a month at the lowest to four to five times per week at the highest. Altogether, the group averaged a usage of between one and two times per week. The students described a number of ways they use AI in the school setting; when prompted with the question "AI helps me to …," their responses included "prepare for tests," "expand my knowledge on various topics, "set a clear plan of action," "get an answer when I'm confused about something," and "have a good alternative resource" when teachers were unavailable (for example, in the evenings or outside school hours).

Students were also asked to share specific ways in which they used AI tools in their classes. A number of students pointed to their usage of AI in English classes, including advanced placement (AP). Students explained that AI, including the school's TrekAI tool, helped them in a variety of ways to understand assignments and readings:

- "So I'm in AP Literature right now, and oftentimes when we get an assignment, I just use it to clarify that I'm answering the prompt or whatever I'm supposed to be writing in the way that the prompt is asking. So it helps clarify definitions for me a lot. And also, I've been able to better understand whether, for example, I've used this rhetorical device correctly in my analysis of a rhetorical situation. I really like to use it in that class specifically, just to clarify that I'm doing what I'm supposed to do."
- "Right now in my English class for doing poetry, we're supposed to break down a poem.... I can feed the poem into the chat, and it'll help if I ask for an analysis of it. And it'll help you understand what [the] poem is trying to say a little better. So I can have a deeper understanding of it to complete [the] assignments."
- "I'm also in AP Language, and I use it a lot to see examples of different essays. Because there are different types of essays, and there are different ways to write commentary and

integrate evidence. And so I'll use it to see how they format it properly."

While it is perhaps not surprising that students find AI tools helpful for English classes, students at GAC also used these tools in many other subjects, including math and science. Their responses for these subjects often pointed to the benefit of using a tool like TrekAI, which incorporates GAC lesson materials and transcripts into its database (see chapter 4 for a more thorough explanation of TrekAI):

- "I use it a lot whenever I have homework sometimes in AP Calculus. I'll use it to break down [a] problem and ask it to guide me in how to approach a problem. Stuff like that. If I don't remember the topic or I'm just having trouble with where to start, I'll sort of use it to guide the difficult questions."
- "In my oceanography class, sometimes if I'm struggling to understand a concept that's being talked about, I'll go back through my notes at the end of the day. And especially what's helpful for me about TrekAI is to plug in a concept that I don't understand. And rather than spreading out the entire answer, it kind of asks more baseline questions that maybe I can answer on my own. It helps build up to the answer for the question that I have."
- "If I don't understand something fully at the beginning of the day, at the end of the day to actually get a baseline understanding of what's happening about my anatomy class concepts, it'll give me what my teacher would say the answer is. And a lot of times if I Google it, [the responses] are either way too specific for what I need to know for a quiz or test or notes in general, or [the Google responses] don't have the answer that I've looked for. So I find it really helpful that we are able to use our teachers' transcripts and what they would have as the answers in class as part of TrekAI."
- "In my psychology class or in physics, it has the transcripts and all the curriculum from the unit in TrekAI, and so I can just ask for practice questions or [a] study guide for a specific part of the unit or the whole unit. [I can ask it to] just do a unit review of twenty questions and it'll give it to me. And

I can do it.... So I find that very useful if the teacher doesn't make a study guide or if I want to practice beyond the study guide."

Beneficial Use by Teachers

In addition to self-directed use of AI, we asked students to describe ways in which teachers have employed AI in helpful ways. Their responses encompassed a wide range of subjects as well as teaching approaches, many of which students found creative and engaging:

- "In our AP U.S. History class, the teacher gives us things called 'ChatGPT Main Idea Logs,' which basically summarize what happens in every chapter of the book we're reading. And it's really helpful, since there's a lot of pages and it's really difficult to memorize entire chapters of the books. So it basically summarizes the main points, like main events [or] really specific details that you need to remember. But there's just so much information in such a large book that it's hard to remember all those details just by reading the book."

- "In my statistics class, we used it to brainstorm for our final project. So you know, you went in with a topic you're interested in. I went in with women's sports. I ended up not even using this topic, but it was just an idea. And I went in ChatGPT and I said, 'Give me five experiments to run tests for women in sports'.... Lots of kids in my class ended up using ideas that they got off ChatGPT."

- "My teacher lets us use it in psychology. We use ChatGPT to help write made-up case studies or something where there's a variable, and you have to go and kind of clarify what's happening in the study or the experiment. And that's been really helpful. [It's] really hard to sit down [with a] piece [of] paper and write your own experiment. So just putting in 'I want to work on something with sleep' [is an] example."

- "It's been helpful in our AP Literature class. Our teacher has used ChatGPT to create an image of a character for a short story—a really fun way to help us visualize the actual story itself."

- "In English class, we'd use it to generate an example of a thesis statement to a prompt or something like that, and that was pretty useful.... You shouldn't miss the thesis point, so I am always, for the prompt, checking if this thesis is accurate."
- "You feed in your essay or assignment along with the grading rubric, and then ask it to, based on the rubric, see what you can improve before you turn it in. That's something that teachers encourage us to do. Sometimes that's even an assignment. That is, on the teacher side, something I think they really like about AI."
- "We were on the book of Revelation in Bible ... and there is a lot of imagery in that book that is very complicated and strange. And so I felt like it was really helpful to be able to feed the commentary through an AI image generator and get a picture of what the Bible was saying back to you. So I feel like that was helpful [in] understanding the book of Revelation better. In my own opinion, I would never have thought to do that for Bible class. So I thought that was [a] great way that they were trying to use it."

Schoolwide Rollout

As described in chapter 4, GAC has taken a deliberate and measured approach to rolling out its TrekAI tool across grades and subject levels. We asked students about the rollout of AI at the school and how teachers directly address the topic of AI in their classes. In general, a positive picture emerged of the ways in which the school scaffolds AI usage for students.

- "We had a trial period at the very beginning of the year, where it was very specific classes [that] were given an opportunity to use it. And it wasn't available to everyone because they're testing it. And I honestly think that's probably the best way to integrate it—to give it to some classes, see how it works, see how much they use it, and then open it up to the rest of the school."
- "In a theology class, one of our unit weeks was about AI. And so that was a very open conversation for our class. We learned what AI is but also what our lenses for thinking about AI [are], and I found that to be super helpful and [it]

made it seem less overwhelming. And then I was able to open that conversation up with my family and my friends and discuss their thoughts on it. That helped me to form my own opinions on it, which I've extended to my personal usage of it as well."
- "Especially in [the] English department, students have been taught about using it.... We do talk about plagiarism in the beginning of [the] year or whenever they have those talks about AI—like how it's okay to use it in certain contexts. But you can't use it in other ways. And they're pretty clear on how you can and can't use it."

Concerns About AI

While we asked students directly about their concerns related to AI, students brought up negative aspects of AI at multiple points during the focus group. These responses indicated that rather than an unvarnished acceptance or enthusiasm about AI, students had a high level of awareness around the possible drawbacks of AI related to learning, integrity, inaccuracy, and creativity.

Learning
- "One of the potential flaws is just straight out regurgitating answers to the questions that students would ask."
- "I think that for some students it is definitely building bad habits by relying on AI, because it's something that's so powerful where you can complete an assignment [quickly].... [But] you're going to get to a point where that's not going to work anymore. And you're going to have bad habits."
- "I have a brother in [middle school], and I hate to say it, but he asks Siri every day how to subtract this problem, just to get quick with it. I'm worried that he's going to forget how to subtract by the time he's in high school, if every day on his homework he asked Siri how to subtract. I feel like that is one of the things you lose if you're asking AI, 'How do I do this problem?' and it tells you. And you're like, oh great, yeah, that's the concept. Let me do my homework real quick, and you get the good grade. [But] when you come

to the test, you can't use AI, and your grades are going to suffer [because] once you get to the test you don't have anything to tell you [the answer] while you're sitting there. I think you lose the ability to learn concepts thoroughly."

Integrity
- "I think there's a very fine line right now [regarding asking questions and getting answers].... How far can you go before it's considered cheating and before you've stepped over the line? You could quickly fall down a rabbit hole where you think you're not cheating, but you actually are."
- "All AIs have their own sort of diction.... A lot of people could recognize it. [But] it's really easy to take the content of what an AI generated and then transform it into your own words. You're still plagiarizing that content.... It's just a simple thing to do. Regarding plagiarism, I think that's a big concern."
- "I remember [one university] application had a big header at the top talking about if you use AI, if we suspect you're using AI, or if we find out that you used AI, your application will be scrapped. But that was the only application I saw that on, and so I'm sure there were hundreds of or thousands of applicants that probably had extremely eloquent and powerful essays that they were able to get from ChatGPT in part or as a whole. Which it's not necessarily unfair, but ... it just doesn't sit right with me—that it's kind of changing the way that something as big as a college application process can work."

Inaccuracy
- "I would say for myself, it's a reliability thing.... I could tell you that I got that answer from ChatGPT. But I don't know where ChatGPT got it, because it just generated it. It could be the wrong answer. Usually it's not, but I mean there have been times where I've known it's just given me the wrong answer, because I can sort of see the right direction of where the right answer would be. And so you

don't exactly know if you're going to get an accurate answer to your question or not."

Creativity
- "It feels very inanimate and impersonal.... It's never going to be able, in a world that I can envision, [to] generate figurative language based off human experience in a way that poems can and real human authors [can].... I take art and I can't imagine integrating ChatGPT into my artwork or into my thought process, because it's not based off human experience in the way that art is. To me, that is honestly scary. And when we had our AI unit in our capstone class, I think pretty much the entire class expressed fear more than excitement about AI, because it does feel so impersonal. And it's this cloud of things that is not based off human experience. And to me I find that pretty jarring, and it is a huge disincentive for me to want to use it."
- "To an extent, you lose unique perspective and creative ideas and independent ideas when it's coming from essentially a probability model.... My dad and I actually had a conversation about this the other day, where he was telling me about an article where college admissions boards were given articles and essays—some written by students and some by AI—and they said they were able to pick out the AI ones because they just went to what they thought was expected and then no more. There weren't more aspects of this, that, you know, [real students] were more passionate about [and] that they would write more about. [AI] couldn't explain how this experience made them feel on a personal human level. And I think if that's the new expectation of script writing for shows, movies, books and articles, and news, [then] that loss of a human aspect to me is quite honestly terrifying. And [it] makes me all the more not want to read those things and watch those things, because it's not personal anymore."

Bible Learning and Faith Formation

Finally, we asked students to share how their use of AI at school connected—or did not connect—to their Bible learning and faith formation. Students agreed that AI could be helpful with Bible knowledge or learning, but not in interpreting the Bible.

- "In Senior Bible at the end of the year, we have projects and presentations that are talking about a lot of difficult and heavy topics. And I'll read the Bible, but I'm not very good at being that person who knows where something is and how it relates to other verses in the Bible. So, ChatGPT and other AI tools have definitely helped me with figuring out what book in the Bible I can use to look in for something, and then how that correlates and relates to other verses in the Bible, because I don't have that vast understanding yet. So, it's definitely helped a lot. And then retaining the fact that this specific concept is more in this book than it is this other book."
- "I think AI would be a lot more beneficial regarding the 'education' of the Bible rather than actually helping faith. For example, we had a recent Bible project where students asked AI to write ten messages that could have happened between God and a Bible character, like say Jeremiah. And it really helped me to get more insight into different characters in the Bible and what decisions they would have made or how they would have reacted to certain things. And it just really helps you understand different characters [and] personalities."
- "I don't think it'd be very useful at all for … interpreting the Bible in any way, because the Bible is very symbolic. It's very symbolic and metaphorical. You have to add the fact that ChatGPT is not humanlike. It's hard for something that's not a living thing to interpret something that's spiritual for you."

When it came to their own faith formation, students were clear that AI could not replace traditional means of discipleship. If anything, students saw AI as reinforcing and deepening their commitment to incarnationally and relationally based ways of growing in their faith.

- "Technology is [a] huge part of our life, and there's aspects [of] constantly being plugged in and online that I really don't enjoy. But I think this year for the first time, I really was able to recognize [that], wow, I don't like this. And for me, that was a big turning point. I think [it's] because I'm not feeling God when I'm online, or, you know, looking at a screen at all. Honestly, I think that was a big turning point in my faith, to realize [that] worship for me isn't watching an online sermon or listening to worship music on my phone. I think worship for me is something I need to feel outside of me. Obviously that looks different for everyone. But it has been an interesting journey, discovering that for myself."
- "There's definitely something to be said about being in a room with a hundred other people and worshiping to the same song and feeling that 'spiritual weather' that people talk about. And I think AI wouldn't ever, at least, in my opinion, replicate that type of feeling where you're like, 'Wow—our God is so good!' All of these other people believe. There's an aspect of faith that is so communal. I don't feel as connected spiritually online as I do when I'm in person for church or when I'm sitting in person with my small group, discussing questions like these: How did this thing that pastor said make you feel? Do you understand this concept, and if you don't, what's preventing you from understanding?"
- "I wouldn't necessarily think of AI as a tool to strengthen my faith. However, I feel just AI as a concept has forced me to challenge my faith, just because it's such a profound concept. And [it] kind of seems to be sort of counterintuitive to faith. I feel like that's something that we really need to talk about, especially in a faith-based school, because I feel like a conversation about what AI is and [its] concepts would help kids to ... broaden their perspective a little. I get the profoundness of it, [so it] kind of forces you to challenge and, I would say, strengthen your faith."

Looking Ahead

This chapter provides a snapshot of a specific moment in time relative to one school's adoption of AI. One student summed up this moment well: "I found that if GAC is giving us an AI to use, that's going to be the safest form. But I still fall back on my textbook or ask my teachers for questions, and I don't even really think about using other AIs, just because it's so new to our education." In the coming months and years, as AI technology continues to develop and familiarity with AI tools increases, students' experiences will undoubtedly change as well.

At the same time, we can be encouraged that students' responses today reveal their thoughtfulness around AI and how it can be utilized best in the classroom, how their learning is shaped (both positively and negatively) by new technology, and even how their faith is formed in the Christian school—most often, independent of technology. When it comes to AI and technology in the Christian school, we have a lot to learn from, and with, our students.

Part III:
Frameworks for Practice

A Framework for Technology Integration in Christian Schools

Shaun Brooker, *Hamilton Christian School*

More than a decade ago in New Zealand, a television advertisement promoted a new chainsaw. Everything about the chainsaw looked impressive until the lumberjack went to cut down the tree in question. The shiny new piece of technology looked light yet powerful and started with the easiest of pulls. Just as the chainsaw was about to do what it was designed to do, the lumberjack pulled the chainsaw back and over his shoulder, then flung it with an almighty force toward the base of the tree—just as he would have with an axe. This chainsaw advertisement is a great visual representation of how new technology is often integrated into the classroom.

It appears that the lumberjack had been convinced to try a chainsaw. Maybe he was encouraged to try this new technology with the promise of being able to cut down a tree with more efficiency, both faster and with less effort. However, the lumberjack, who could clearly swing an item with great force, was only comfortable with the way he cut down trees with an older technology (an axe).

In a way, the lumberjack could be encouraged. At least, some would say, he gave the new technology a try. However, in this scenario, he will likely put the new technology aside and revert back to an axe. And this is understandable. If the lumberjack was comfortable only by swinging an object against a tree to cut it down, a chainsaw is not the right technology for him.

Chainsaws are not the only technology that require users to change their approach and actions. If you usually bake a cake for forty-five minutes in an oven and try to do the same in a microwave, the cake will be destroyed and you will think the new technology is unhelpful. If you turn on your air conditioning in the car on a hot day and keep your windows down—because that is what you have always done on a hot day—you'll probably conclude the additional fuel consumption for a technology that has little to no effect on the car's internal climate isn't worth it. Actually, in these examples, because of how they are being used, the impact of the new technology is far from neutral—it is negative.

This scene has played itself out time and time again for more than a decade as schools implement new technology strategies. Just like a lumberjack moving from using an axe to a chainsaw, teachers who are not equipped well or simply do not want to change their pedagogy are left frustrated with new technology, and it impedes teaching and learning. And their argument rings true: Their classroom is better off without the technology if they are not prepared to change.

New technology requires a new pedagogy to realize all the technology has to offer. If we fail to implement a new design for learning alongside a new technology, that new technology will, at best, have a neutral but costly effect on students. Most likely, however, the net effect will be negative.

This chapter considers three aspects of technology integration in education:
1. It presents a tool to assess and plan for the use of technology in a meaningful way.
2. It explores how the questions we ask about technology integration will limit or extend how technology can transform learning experiences.
3. It explores the use of artificial intelligence (AI), specifically in the context of Christian education: the good, the bad, and the maybe.

The Device Multiuse Matrix (dMatrix): A Tool for Meaningful Technology Integration and Review

Like the chainsaw, which made an impact on the forestry industry, new technologies can positively impact the learning process if used well. To assess if a technology is being used meaningfully in the classroom, it is essential to consider student outcomes in the future and the use of a reflective tool in the present. The Device Multiuse Matrix (dMatrix) is offered as a tool to help create meaningful use of technology and to reflect on how students have engaged with technology in the past.

At its core, the dMatrix considers how digital technologies are used in the educational environment, expressed through the four Cs against an expression of Dr. Ruben Puentedura's SAMR model (Puentedura 2006). The SAMR model is a continuum of digital technology use, from substituting pen and paper to redefining the educational experience. To understand the dMatrix, it is essential to understand both the four Cs and the SAMR model.

The SAMR Model

The dMatrix uses an expression of the SAMR model. SAMR is an acronym for substitution, augmentation, modification, and redefinition. Each stage represents a deepening impact that technology can have in the classroom. Puentedura asserts that the first two stages, substitution and augmentation, represent technology use that enhances the learning process, whereas the third and fourth stages represent technology that transforms the learning process (table 1).

Table 1. The SAMR Model

Enhancement	Substitution	Technology allows for direct tool substitution with no functional improvement.
	Augmentation	Technology allows for direct tool substitution with functional improvement.
Transformation	Modification	Technology allows for significant task redesign.
	Redefinition	Technology allows for the creation of new tasks previously inconceivable.

The following is a very high-level view of all stages to explain them and how they apply to the dMatrix.

- **Substitution (SAMR Stage 1).** At the substitution stage, digital technology is used to simply substitute pen and paper with digital technology. Often, this is where the task was developed for a pen-and-paper activity, and if a student has a device, they can use it for the same task. Fundamental to this stage is that the task at hand could be completed either by using pen and paper or through digital means. This would include students typing a letter to send to an author, reading a PDF on a device, or filling in missing words on a Google doc.
- **Augmentation (SAMR Stage 2).** Teachers and students can use technologies to add value to substitution activities. Where this is done intentionally, the task is augmented by technology. Such a task could include allowing students to

use a spelling checker or applications that automatically mark students' work. In both cases, students get feedback and assistance through the technology in a way that they would not get if they completed the task by using pen and paper.
- **Modification (SAMR Stage 3).** The modification stage is the first of the two stages where new tasks are created for students because of what digital technologies make possible. For example, teachers could have students create movies or podcasts to show their understanding of a new concept. They could also use GarageBand to introduce students to songwriting and composition or have students create a song to unpack a theme in a book they are reading in class. Digital technology can complement teacher instruction through the use of a library of videos that students can watch so they can learn about a new concept in multiple ways and not be limited to learning only when the teacher is standing in front of the class.
- **Redefinition (SAMR Stage 4).** In the fourth stage, a school's use of technology causes educators to rethink many aspects of their operation and how learning is structured. Whereas the modification stage equates to the transformation of individual educational tasks, the redefinition stage refers to the transformation of schools. The implication of new hardware (such as one-to-one devices) has had a moderate impact on the structure and function of schools. However, the new chapter of artificial intelligence will likely have a significant effect. Recently, a school in Texas named Alpha School opened with no teachers—only students and adults who are "coaches." The teacher is AI.

The Four Cs

While knowing the difference between the four stages of SAMR is important, educators should realize that the dMatrix also incorporates a continuum of device use. Whereas the SAMR model describes technology's transformational effect on learning, the four Cs are a way to categorize the different tasks that students engage with on digital technologies—how students learn new information, engage with content, express their new learnings, and more. In general, most ways students use digital technologies meaningfully in the classroom can be categorized under four headings, all beginning with the letter *C*:

- content creation;
- content consumption;
- concept reinforcement; and
- communication

Content Creation

Students create content to show their teacher or a more extensive audience what they understand. The function of writing is such a central part of the education world, yet once a student departs from education, writing extensive essays to present their point of view or learnings or to record observations is primarily replaced by the need to communicate orally. But to this day, writing continues to be a fundamental measure of knowledge. In a world where many students are disengaged with the writing process, it is likely that many of them are now living out self-fulfilled prophecies that they are not good at writing. While still respecting the place that writing has in education, students can use digital technologies to create content that showcases their ideas and learning without the limitations of functional writing.

Content creation on digital technologies includes video making, podcast production, blogging, vlogging, animation, slideshow presentations, song production, and more. Once students have expressed their ideas digitally, these outputs can be used, if needed, to guide their written tasks. Many students, but not all, will engage much more meaningfully in sharing their ideas and learnings when asked to produce a three-minute video than when being asked to write a six-hundred-word essay. Not only does digital technology provide many ways for students to create content, but it can also provide for more meaningful tasks where the audience is more extensive than just the teacher. Yes, privacy issues need to be addressed, but when done successfully, work can be published to other students, the wider community, and even the worldwide audience. It is very motivating for students when a class is publishing a book of short stories or releasing a worship album. Many students rise to the occasion and find motivation that is not there with more text-based assignments.

Content Consumption

When a student gleans information from a device in any form, the process is referred to as content consumption; they are consuming content from the device. In a deviceless learning environment, students consume content through books, papers, the teacher, and each other. Digital technologies both complement and create new opportunities for content consumption. A device can complement the current classroom procedures when the teacher shares digitally with students copies of the papers or texts used in class or uploads videos explaining a new concept to a shared location.

Even these two simple, almost substitutional tasks can add value to student learning. Papers shared digitally are less likely to be lost and, therefore, are more readily available to all students for reference when studying for exams. Secondly, sharing a video of the teacher explaining a concept to a shared drive allows students to watch the video multiple times until they understand—all the while not requiring them to repeatedly ask the teacher the same question in front of their peers.

However, digital technology can create more opportunities for students to consume information. Using resources already available online, teachers can curate a treasure trove of resources students have on hand to understand new concepts. Songs, videos, and podcasts have already been mentioned. But there are many more resources, including educational websites, infographics, online libraries, and audiobooks, to name a few. One important note about using the internet or AI for content consumption: Students need to be guided in their use and interpretation of both. Teachers who navigate this well curate websites and resources intentionally for their students. The freedom to explore the internet is reserved for a time when students are mature enough to know how not to be distracted, dis-informed, and desensitized. Teachers who harness digital technologies well can create more powerful and effective learning environments, marked by opportunities for students to be more meaningfully engaged, than teachers who use only text-based activities.

Concept Reinforcement

Digital technologies can engage students in what otherwise could become uninspired and repetitive tasks regarding concept reinforcement. When students learn a new concept, they must practice it often. Countless digital applications gamify these tasks in a way that challenges and motivates students to do more. Furthermore, such applications usually give students instant feedback on their responses and allow them to make immediate adjustments to their process or thinking. This is opposed to when they have a task of answering twenty questions that the teacher marks at the end of the session, which means that students may have misunderstood one part of the new concept and will only know to change their thinking once they learn they are wrong. By this stage, they have repeated the process nineteen times more than they would have with instant feedback.

Many concept reinforcement applications will offer students "help" when they get several questions wrong. Where the concept reinforcement application is designed with school in mind, it is usually loaded with many data points or analytics to give teachers easy access to what their students can and cannot do, thereby empowering them to design lessons meaningfully and target teaching where needed.

Communication

Digital technologies open up a whole new world in communication and education. While traditional aspects of communication can still be completed through digital technologies, such as communicating with parents and pen pals and giving feedback to students, the internet has brought many new opportunities. Classes now video call schools in other parts of the world to understand different cultures better—much better than from a book. Groups of students communicate in real-time with astronauts and authors to ask questions and better understand what motivates them or how they do what they do—a much more authentic and engaging process than reading about astronauts and authors. Students can also make their work available to parents much more freely and gain feedback from them in a way that makes the home much closer to the school.

Putting SAMR and the Four Cs Together

The dMatrix (Brooker 2016) is a tool that has married the SAMR model and the four Cs. Teachers can reflect on their use of technology to add value to the learning process. On the dMatrix, teachers plot the many different ways that their students have used digital technologies in class or for homework. Once all the digital tasks are plotted on the matrix, it is easy to see where technology is used as a substitution for pen and paper or is transforming learners' experience in education (table 2).

Table 2. The Device Multiuse Matrix (dMatrix)

Toward Transformation				
Simply Substitution				
	Content Creation	Content Consumption	Concept Reinforcement	Communication

The goal is not to have all the tasks sitting in the higher transformation stages of SAMR but to know where technology is being used well and where it is not. If a task is designed for pen and paper, and there is no functional benefit for completing it on a device, it should remain a pen-and-paper activity. Where gaps on the matrix are found, teachers can then ask more pointed questions to their colleagues or online to create activities that better realize the potential that digital technology has in education.

Asking the Right Question

A final comment about implementing digital technologies meaningfully in the educational process: When teachers consider digital technology integration in their classroom, they will ask one of two questions.

1. How do I use digital technology in my syllabus? or,
2. What can I do with my syllabus because of digital technology?

The teacher who asks the first question will always default to activities that are a substitute for pen and paper. And, like the lumberjack, they will most likely give up on any new technology because it is easier and more effective to use older, more traditional technologies. However, the teacher who asks the second question is about to enter a world of new possibilities for the students. The syllabus is still important; what their students need to learn should be protected, but how they engage in the learning is about to be transformed.

A final thought on using digital technologies in the educational environment is to look for ways students can work together on a single device. One criticism of digital technologies is that they close students off from those around them. This is true. While connecting students to the proverbial world, they can be completely isolated from those immediately around them. Educators have the opportunity to design learning with devices in a way that causes students to share, discuss, and collaborate in groups. One student in a group can be responsible for recording the discussion on a device and can easily share those notes with others.

Artificial Intelligence

Closing your eyes will not make it go away; artificial intelligence is coming, and it will make waves, not ripples. Artificial intelligence can and likely will impact how we teach, learn, capture moments, write farewell poems, prepare for an interview, and even how we think of ourselves as productive humans. And all of that is likely with just the power of artificial intelligence as we know it today—to say nothing of future technologies.

The introduction of AI in education is often compared to the introduction of calculators in the past (Chun 2023). While there are some parallels, a significant difference is that AI has the ability to influence decisions and, therefore, people. Yes, calculators in classrooms took some time to digest, and some people stood firm on their ground that their introduction would have no positive outcomes for student learning. However, once they were embraced as a tool that students could access for the rest of their lives, the curriculum changed, and pedagogy adapted, allowing them to solve problems they could only have dreamed of in the past. This is to say nothing of the graphic calculator.

And AI will have (if it hasn't already) a considerable impact not only in teaching and learning in the humanities but across most, if not all, curriculum areas. AI has already infiltrated the arts, sciences, and social sciences, and it is coming for Bible class. As students seek answers from the Scripture through the use of AI, they are being presented with some truth and some non-truths. AI does not always answer with the whole truth, and to be frank, it does not care, and it does not even know.

Our students must have a sound understanding of the truth in Scripture before engaging with AI in areas of spirituality. Moreover, as Christians, we must guard against the loss of wisdom. We should use AI to complement and stimulate our thinking and creative endeavors. AI is a powerful tool, but it is a powerful tool that must be harnessed for the good it can do. Educators, especially Christian educators, must equip students to not outsource their thinking to machines. The possibility of a loss of metacognition is real, as is a continual deviation from what is truth. Not surprisingly, Proverbs, the book of wisdom, has a word or two about guarding wisdom and understanding (Proverbs 4:1–9, 19:8). AI needs to be unpacked in an environment that is saturated in mature, godly wisdom.

When used wisely, AI can have a positive impact on learning and teaching. This includes the following:

1. *Helping students improve an essay that they have written.* In the world today, not every child has a parent at home to read their school papers and give an opinion on how to improve their work. Children with this help at home have a significant advantage over those who do not. AI can level the playing field for all students by giving them such feedback.
2. *Assisting a student who struggles with writing articulately to share their ideas.* While schools promote critical thinking, ideas are generally only valued if they are articulated and formatted in a particular way. In the world outside of education, ideas are valued above grammar. I often reflect on the fact that nobody has ever asked me to write for their magazine or website because my spelling is perfect and my paragraphs are so eloquent. An exciting aspect of AI as a tool is that it can improve the value of the ideas of learners who struggle with writing up to the value of those who can spell and sequence words well.
3. *Transforming the way we measure knowledge.* It is becoming increasingly difficult to detect plagiarism. Due to AI's impact on text-based assessment, high schools and colleges must reconsider their assessment models. As with the preceding point, this might create significantly more accessibility for learners who are less able to express their ideas in a written format.
4. *Accessing a vast knowledge bank of ideas for how to design learning for all learners.* Asking AI how to adapt a lesson plan for a student who is blind, has dyslexia, needs enrichment, or is struggling to understand a concept will yield an endless number of suggestions. AI will even differentiate your lessons if you ask the right questions. All this can be done in

nanoseconds, whereas it could take hours to do through just searching the internet.

Technologies, including artificial intelligence, need to prioritize the development of students' thinking deeply. Used well, digital technologies will open new pathways for students to learn and to present their ideas and learnings. Digital technologies have the potential to not only engage more students more meaningfully in the learning process but also provide more support for them—and for their teachers. However, technology, especially artificial intelligence, has the potential to do a lot of damage to the learning process, as well as to students' understanding and grasp of truth. Christian educators need wisdom to guide their students in an AI-driven world.

In Christian education, we need to take dominion over technology, to not be scared by it, and certainly not ignore it. Students who start school today will leave high school around the year 2037. Who has any idea what the world will look like then and what technological tools they will be using? Whatever the future brings, we need people who know truth and can think deeply about the world around them—using the tools available to them with great wisdom and embracing all the means within their reach to fulfill the Great Commission's call to make disciples of all nations.

Digital Well-Being and the Christian School
Christina Crook, *JOMO*

We can remember a time before the internet. They can't.

I once spent a slow afternoon experiencing *Age of You*, a vast collection of photography, sculpture, video, and text at the Museum of Contemporary Art Toronto. In one immersive experience, artists sought to make sense of the global shifts we've undergone as digital technology has furiously reshaped our world—more often for the better, but sometimes for the worse. The exhibit revealed how every part of our lives has been transformed, disrupted, or made obsolete, including our relationships with ourselves—our own knowing—and our need for one another. The collection showed how, in almost every online context, our attention has been in service of someone else, someone who stood to gain by us consuming more information, products, connections, and likes while, out of sight, they consumed more and more of our data.

The curators, which included Douglas Coupland (writer, visual artist, and designer who became the voice of a generation with his novel *Generation X*), intended to urge viewers to consider how digital capitalism (capitalism conducted through the internet) has forced the self to become more extreme—a performance, inauthentic in its portrayal. Just look at TikTok: When it comes to views, spectacle beats substance every time. And just look around—you'll see signs of the extreme everywhere. Extreme fear of what's happening to your personal data. Extreme presentations of self in service of online follower growth. Extreme political polarization. Extreme dis-ease in relationships and communities, online and off, as the lines between the real and unreal (thanks to AI, deep fakes, and fake news) blur beyond recognition. This is the world we and our youth inhabit.

Student Well-Being: In Jeopardy

Today's adolescents are living in the era of "everywhere is anywhere is anything is everything"—a time when AI blurs the lines of reality and digital capitalism drives the terms of social engagement to the extent that students are left wanting—wanting for something real. "Adults can't really imagine how bad kids feel," says youth advocate Sean Killingsworth (2023), creator of the Reconnect movement. "In the social wasteland that exists in schools today, you're already rejected before you say anything."

His feelings mirror what I heard in interviews with undergraduate and graduate students at Virginia Tech during the 2022/2023 academic year. In a series of in-person conversations, students confided, "I'm here because I am on my tech twenty-four hours a day," "I'd love to throw my phone in the ocean, but I need to be a productive person in the world," "I was told before I arrived on campus that there is too much tech. I was told I have to 'adapt or die.'"

These students' sentiments merge with the insights researchers Jean Twenge and Jonathan Haidt have been mapping with their global collaborative review of studies related to social media and smartphones' impact on adolescent mental health. As Haidt (2023) highlighted in the *After Babel* Substack publication,

> A big story last week was the partial release of the CDC's bi-annual Youth Risk Behavior Survey, which showed that most teen girls (57%) now say that they experience persistent sadness or hopelessness (up from 36% in 2011), and 30% of teen girls now say that they have seriously considered suicide (up from 19% in 2011).... The big surprise in the CDC data is that COVID didn't have much effect on the overall trends, which just kept marching on as they have since around [the emergence of smartphones and social media in] 2012.

The result? A global adolescent mental health crisis evidenced by decreased social connectedness and increased anxiety and disengagement on campuses around the world.

In fall 2023, my digital wellness company, JOMO, began a long-term collaboration with the wellness department of Virginia Tech. Through a close reading of the university's most recent College Health Assessment and conducting more than a dozen long-form faculty and student interviews, my colleague Laurie Fritsch and I identified three key digital trends on campus:

1. **Procrastination abounds.** Seventy-five percent of students reported challenges with procrastination that causes moderate to high distress and negatively affects academic performance and progress toward a degree.
2. **Hooked on the internet.** Mindless tech consumption (social media scrolling, binge-watching) and FOMO are norms among teens and young adults, leading to anxiety, distraction, loneliness, and, in some cases, physical harm.
3. **Overwhelmed by notifications.** Lack of digital boundaries leads to interrupted focus and flow in deep work. As one student put it, "Getting a notification at night is like your professor walking up and knocking on your front door."

Is this what students want? No, says Killingsworth (2023), who has started a small unplugged event series on Florida campuses: "We don't actually want our phones or Snapchat. What we want is real connection, but that doesn't happen in the new ecosystem. Everything that naturally breeds real connection has been lost."

Educator Well-Being: Not Much Better

The story is not much different for adults. Our days are full. For most of us, from the moment we wake up in the morning, our days are rife with noise, busyness, and rushing. At the end of the day, we are tired. So very exhausted. Can you relate to any of the feelings below that adults have articulated?

- "I'm tired of trying to keep it all together. My team needs me. My spouse needs me. My kids need me. I feel like I am already living with a wall of regret."
- "I'm exhausted. I'm on 24-7. I feel like I can't turn off because if I do my career will slow down and my boss will think I'm … and I will miss my dentist appointment and I'll never get my side hustle off the ground … and I won't know about my friend's new puppy and …"
- "I come home from work feeling numb. The only thing I have energy for is scrolling and Netflix. And more Netflix. And more Instagram. And more Facebook. At the same

time. I've been on social media long enough to know it's a waste of time but I. CAN. NOT. STOP. I don't know what else to do."

As adults, we want to have a simple lifestyle, but we also want all the comforts of modern life. We want to have the depth afforded by solitude, but we also do not want to miss anything. We want to have time to think, but we also want to watch television, read, talk to friends, and go out. "Small wonder," writes Ronald Rolheiser (2014) in his book *The Holy Longing*, "life is so often a trying enterprise and we are often tired and pathologically overextended. Medieval philosophy had a dictum that said: Every choice is a thousand renunciations. To choose one thing is to turn one's back on many others" (25). It takes a powerful no to say a powerful yes.

Keys to Lifelong Well-Being

In 1938, Harvard University started following 268 undergraduate students in the longest-running study of human development in history. The goal was to determine what factors contribute most strongly to human flourishing. The researchers measured their subjects on everything: personality type, IQ, drinking habits, family relationships. Everything. The head of the study, psychiatrist George Eman Vaillant, published the findings from the study, which is still ongoing, in *Triumphs of Experience* (2015). The factor of life success Vaillant refers to most often is the powerful correlation between the warmth of your relationships and your health and happiness in your later years.

If there's any part of you rolling your eyes right now, you're not alone. In 2009, Vaillant's insistence on the importance of this variable was challenged, and he returned to the data for reanalysis. Not only did he find that he had accurately correlated the quality of relationships to well-being, but he determined that it was even more closely linked than he had previously thought.

Vaillant measured warm relationships as having close friends, maintaining contact with family, and being active in social organizations. Vaillant explained, "It was the capacity for intimate relationships that predicted flourishing in all aspects of these subjects' lives." After seventy-five years and twenty million dollars spent on research, Vaillant concluded that the key to human flourishing can be summed up in five simple words: "Happiness is love. Full stop."

We must remember that at its core, technology is not about love. On an average day, we spend more time with our digital products and platforms than we do with any single human being. Because of this, the three sirens of consumerism—comfort, control, and convenience—have seeped into our thinking. They shape the way we think about relationships. They shape the way we learn and work. They may even shape the way we build community and educate. But what is the human cost?

It is true that creating—making anything worthwhile—whether it be a family, a resilient mind, a vocation, a marriage, or a vibrant neighborhood, doesn't work like that. There's nothing efficient about it. Here is what I'm getting at: The tech that shapes our lives is at odds with the way humans actually work. At our core, we and our students are after one thing: love. Meaning and belonging. But here's the thing: Love is the opposite of comfort, control, and convenience. The way we experience love is through relationship, and relationships aren't easy—they're effortful. Control and efficiency—the promises of our tech-obsessed world—aren't going to get us where we want to go.

Think about it. The things you are most proud of in life—the child you are raising, the marathon you completed, the major project you hit out of the park—these required all of you: all of your attention, all of your love, all of your courage, and all of the risk. Could you control it? No. Were you all in? Of course you were. It is in these great effortful pursuits that we experience not only the outer reaches of our abilities but our limits, which require us to rely on others and deepen our love of the people and projects that mean the most to us. They're good burdens. The burdensome part of these activities is actually just the task of getting across a threshold of effort. As soon as you have crossed the threshold, the burden disappears.

It's what you were made for. "What happens when technology moves beyond lifting genuine burdens and starts freeing us from burdens that we should not want to be rid of?" asks philosopher Albert Borgmann (1984) in *Technology and the Character of Contemporary Life*. "If we believe that we, as humans, were created for relationship and meaningful work, work that provides for families and serves neighbors, work that engages our bodies and creative faculties, then it follows that we would value a certain kind of burden," he explains.

He called them "good burdens," commitments that tether us to people and the physical world. Like the burden of preparing a meal and getting everyone to show up at the table and sit down, or the burden of reading poetry to one another or going for a walk after dinner, or the burden of letter writing—gathering our thoughts, setting them down in a way that will be remembered and cherished and perhaps passed on to our grandchildren. "These are the activities that have been obliterated by the readily available entertainment offered by TV"—and every other screen in the twenty-first-century world, he states.

Stepping out of your algorithm is essential to moving out of a set position and into relationship. Mary Clark Moschella, professor of pastoral care and counseling at Yale Divinity School, once told me this: "The joy of being in relationship is that we step outside of ourselves." This is the invitation we must offer our students—the reclamation of effortful living as the path to well-being. We must teach and give our students opportunities to practice channeling their energies online and off toward good burdens—caring relationships, community, and creative projects that bring joy.

Schoolwide Solutions for Digital Well-Being

One of the most significant discoveries working with schools to help them build a digital well-being culture is that problematic technology use is not just an individual student problem; it's systemic. For example, at Virginia Tech, students must use two-factor authentication with their phone to log into Canvas, Virginia Tech's learning management system. Consequently, students are tethered to their smartphones by the university's design. We began experimenting with classroom prompts to "two-factor now and put your phone away," and teaching students how to turn on twenty-four-hour or seven-day factoring to remove the digital hurdle.

One study found that students who can see the screen of a multitasker's laptop (but were not multitasking themselves) score up to 17 percent lower on comprehension than those who had no distracting view. The research on banning smartphones at schools points to higher test scores, less anxiety, and more exercise. Teachers in the United Kingdom are in the process of banning mobile phone use during the school day. Experts suggest that the United States consider doing the same.

Some of the best ideas for digital well-being on campus come directly from students. Here are some of the ideas we heard:

- "I would love it if teachers would begin with 'How to Succeed' in each class. Set clear expectations regarding homework, due dates, communication, how much time we should spend on our work, and how to study well for that class."
- "Take away phones! Force people out of their comfort zones. It's super connecting."
- "I think phones only hurt people when you are with people. They can make you miss what's right in front of you. I need to find a way NOT to have the world at my fingertips."

Consider your own school. What are the digital well-being needs you see? What are the opportunities for increasing student social engagement and academic focus? Technology policies and student agreements only get us so far. To create a digital wellness culture, introduce campus approaches to technology that support student connectedness, mental health, and academic focus. This involves five related efforts:

1. **Establish digital well-being as a strategic priority.** Imagine a flourishing campus where students, faculty, and staff prioritize in-person connection over digital distraction. Involve students, staff, and families in the envisioning process.
2. **Create screen-free spaces.** Build new healthy social norms that make it okay to not be on your phone. Off-topic device use impedes academic performance. Keeping phones out of sight can improve concentration, increase the ability to retain information, and help reduce stress.
3. **Offer digital well-being education.** Help students think critically about technology use and the positive impacts of reducing screen time. Wraparound awareness-building, inspiration, and education for students and families help youth learn and practice digital well-being strategies to help them thrive on campus and off. This hot topic is an excellent

opportunity to codevelop curriculum and school campaigns for students, by students.
4. **Establish and revisit clear, consistent policies regularly.** This should be a living document, revised often, with student consultation, and tied to the "why."
5. **Lead from your values.** During two campus visits in the Metro Vancouver area in early 2024, Christian high school students shared that their school's community values helped them make better decisions online, saying, "The community life values are what makes this a really good school community," and, "The values at our school help us make better decisions, like not making light of actually bad content."

Living the "Examen"-ed Life

Our online environments—where our students (and often we as adults) now spend the lion's share of waking hours—can be controlled, whereas the natural world and human experience are intrinsically unpredictable. A meaningful life may offer a mix of suffering and joy, filled with many unknowns, much disorder, and assured valleys along with the mountaintops. That's why once we've tasted the pleasures of control, it's difficult to turn away. Further, our websites and apps generally do not encourage reflection; instead, they urge us to consume—more email, more goods, and more information. Screen time, when used at length mindlessly, falls firmly in the life-taking column. But, the truth is, consumption is not our great and final goal. We were made for more.

So, if we are to help ourselves and our students find balance in a wired world, we have to help them find something better, something that allows them to experience life both meaningfully and reflectively. The truth is that the easiest way to get off technology is to find something better to do and lean into it. We need to invite ourselves and our students to be attentive to those life-giving people, projects, and pastimes and to make more space for them.

One practical way to do this is through the practice of the Examen. The Examen, developed by Saint Ignatius Loyola (1491–1556), the founder of the Jesuits, is a daily contemplative practice intended to help people become aware of the presence of God in their life. A simplified version of the Examen is this: At the end of each day, ask, "For what today am I most grateful? and "For what am I least grateful?" Put another way: "What today was most life-giving?" and "What was most life-taking?"

Saint Ignatius believed that the key to a healthy spirituality was to find God in all things and work constantly to gain freedom in our lives to cooperate with God's will—that meant seeking the good and the life-giving, in the belief that God leads us to do more of those things that bring delight and peace, and fewer of those that bring heaviness, less of that which takes life. Over time, this centuries-old practice of reflection can be a powerful tool. In the age of AI, it is more important than ever to help ourselves and our students stay grounded in reality, and the Examen is one of the simplest and most effective daily spiritual practices to accomplish this. What was the most life-giving or life-taking experience for me today? This question connects them to their lived experience—one that no one can manipulate, deep fake, or profit from.

Through practices like the Examen, we can connect with the good burdens in our lives—our commitments to people and creative work that shape the beating, breathing world. This is our surest path to joy. A life of passive consumption is not what we were made for. We were made for more. We were made to love. Let's show our students it's worth the effort.

REFERENCES

Introduction: Framing the AI Question

Brue, Ethan J., Derek C. Schuurman, and Steven H. VanderLeest. 2022. *A Christian Field Guide to Technology for Engineers and Designers*. Westmont, IL: IVP.

Gordon, Cindy. 2023. "How Are Educators Reacting to ChatGPT?" *Forbes.com*. https://www.forbes.com/sites/cindygordon/2023/04/30/how-are-educators-reacting-to-chat-gpt.

Lennox, John C. 2020. *2084: Artificial Intelligence and the Future of Humanity*. Grand Rapids, MI: Zondervan Reflective.

Montenegro-Rueda, Marta, et al. 2023. "Impact of the Implementation of ChatGPT in Education: A Systematic Review." *Computers* 12, no. 8 (July 25).

Swaner, Lynn E. and Rian Djita. 2024. *Navigating AI in Christian Schools*. Colorado Springs, CO: ACSI and Hamilton, ON: Cardus.

Part I: Philosophy and Research

Chapter 1: AI in Education: Villain, Savior, or Something Else?

Anderson, Margo. 2023. "'AI Pause' Open Letter Stokes Fear and Controversy." https://spectrum.ieee.org/ai-pause-letter-stokes-fear.

Andreessen, Marc. 2023 "Why AI Will Save the World." https://a16z.com/ai-will-save-the-world/.

Arnold, Kenneth C., April M. Volzer, and Noah G. Madrid. 2021. "Generative Models Can Help Writers without Writing for Them." IUI Workshop on Human-AI Co-Creation with Generative Models.

Bavinck, Herman, John Bolt, and John Vriend. 2003. *Reformed Dogmatics, Vol. 1: Prolegomena*. Ada, MI: Baker Academic.

Bender, Emily et al. 2021. "On the Dangers of Stochastic Parrots: Can Language Models Be Too Big?" In Proceedings of the 2021 ACM Conference on Fairness, Accountability, and Transparency (FAccT '21: 2021 ACM Conference on Fairness, Accountability, and Transparency, Virtual Event Canada: ACM, 2021).

Brooks, Frederick P. 1995. *The Mythical Man-Month: Essays on Software Engineering*, Anniversary Edition. Reading, MA: Addison-Wesley Professional.

Colvin, Jeff. 2016. *Humans are Underrated: What High Achievers Know That Brilliant Machines Never Will*. Brentford, UK: Portfolio Books Ltd.

Dakhel, Arghavan Moradei et al. 2022. "GitHub Copilot AI Pair Programmer: Asset or Liability?" https://doi.org/10.48550/ARXIV.2206.15331.

Ellul, Jacques. 1989. *The Presence of the Kingdom*. Colorado Springs, CO: Helmers and Howard Publishers.

Fortuna, Jeff, Derek C. Schuurman, and David Capson. 2002. "A Comparison of PCA and ICA for Object Recognition under Varying Illumination." *Object Recognition Supported by User Interaction for Service Robots*, vol. 3 (16th International Conference on Pattern Recognition, Quebec City, Que., Canada: IEEE Computer Society), 11–15.

Horvitz, Eric. 2022. "On the Horizon: Interactive and Compositional Deepfakes." Proceedings of the 2022 International Conference on Multimodal Interaction, 653–661.

House, Bryan W., David W. Capson, and Derek C. Schuurman. 2011. "Towards Real-Time Sorting of Recyclable Goods Using Support Vector Machines" in Proceedings of the 2011 IEEE International Symposium on Sustainable Systems and Technology (2011 IEEE International Symposium on Sustainable Systems and Technology (ISSST), Chicago, IL, USA: IEEE), 1–6.

Ito, Aki. 2023. "The End of Coding as We Know It." *Business Insider*, April 26, 2023. https://www.businessinsider.com/chatgpt-ai-technology-end-of-coding-software-developers-jobs-2023-4.

Jackson, Joshua C. et al. 2023. "Exposure to Automation Explains Religious Declines." Proceedings of the National Academy of Sciences 120, no. 34 (August 22, 2023).

Jakesch, Maurice et al. 2023. "Co-Writing with Opinionated Language Models Affects Users' Views." Proceedings of the 2023 CHI Conference on Human Factors in Computing Systems.

Langston, Jennifer. 2017. "Lip-syncing Obama: New tools turn audio clips into realistic video." *UW News*, July 7, 2017. https://www.washington.edu/news/2017/07/11/lip-syncing-obama-new-tools-turn-audio-clips-into-realistic-video/.

Lewis, C.S. 2014. *God in the Dock: Essays on Theology and Ethics*, ed. Walter Hooper. Grand Rapids, MI: Wm. B. Eerdmans.

Metz, Cade. 2023. "Chatbots May 'Hallucinate' More Often Than Many Realize." *The New York Times*, November 6, 2023. https://www.nytimes.com/2023/11/06/technology/chatbots-hallucination-rates.html.

Negroponte, Nicholas. 1996. *Being Digital*. New York: Knopf Doubleday.

O'Neil, Cathy. 2016. *Weapons of Math Destruction: How Big Data Increases Inequality and Threatens Democracy*. New York: Crown.

Schneier, Bruce and Nathan E. Sanders. 2023. "Six Ways That AI Could Change Politics." *MIT Technology Review*, July 28, 2023.

Schuurman, Derek C. 2019. *Shaping a Digital World: Faith, Culture and Computer Technology*. Westmont, IL: IVP Academic.

Schuurman, Derek C. 2022. "Technology and the Opening Chapters of Genesis." https://christianscholars.com/technology-and-the-opening-chapters-of-genesis/.

Shanahan, Murray. 2024. "Talking about Large Language Models," *Communications of the ACM* 67, no. 2 (February).

Tamkin, Alex et al. 2021. "Understanding the Capabilities, Limitations, and Societal Impact of Large Language Models." https://arxiv.org/abs/2102.02503.

References

Weizenbaum, Joseph. 1976. *Computer Power and Human Reason: From Judgment to Calculation*. New York: W.H. Freeman & Co.

Wolters, Albert M. 2005. *Creation Regained: Biblical Basics for a Reformational Worldview*, 2nd ed. Grand Rapids, MI: Eerdmans.

Wood, W. Jay and William Jay Wood. 1998. *Epistemology: Becoming Intellectually Virtuous*. Downers Grove, IL: InterVarsity Press.

Chapter 2: A Biblical Framework for Understanding and Responding to Artificial Intelligence

Bailey, Justin A. 2022. *Interpreting Your World: Five Lenses for Engaging Theology and Culture*. Grand Rapids, MI: Baker Academic.

Crouch, Andy. 2022. *The Life We're Looking For: Reclaiming Relationship in a Technological World*. New York: Convergent Books.

Darrach, B. 1970. "Meet Shaky: The First Electronic Person." *Life Magazine* 69, no. 21: 58B–68B.

Pagliery, Jose and Hope King. 2016. "Computers Will Overtake Us When They Learn to Love, Says Futurist Ray Kurzweil." https://money.cnn.com/2016/03/08/technology/ray-kurzweil-artificial-intelligence.

Postman, Neil. 1993. *Technopoly: The Surrender of Culture to Technology*. New York: Knopf.

Thompson, Clive. 2013. *Smarter Than You Think: How Technology Is Changing Our Minds for the Better*. New York: Penguin.

Turkle, Sherry. 2011. *Alone Together: Why We Expect More from Technology and Less from Each Other*. Philadelphia: Basic Books.

Wolters, Albert M. 2005. *Creation Regained: Biblical Basics for a Reformational Worldview*, 2nd ed. Grand Rapids, MI: Eerdmans.

Chapter 3: The State of AI in Christian Schools: Findings from Research

Cheng, Albert, Rian Djita, and David Hunt. 2022. "Many Educational Systems, A Common Good: An International Comparison of American, Canadian, and Australian Graduates from the Cardus Education Survey." https://www.cardus.ca/research/education/reports/many-educational-systems-a-common-good/.

Foster, Richard N. 1986. *Innovation: The Attacker's Advantage*. New York: Summit Books.

Grubbs, Michael. 2023. "The Inflection Point of Generative AI." https://www.linkedin.com/pulse/inflection-point-generative-ai-michael-grubbs/.

Nasir, Umar. 2023. "The Mass Adoption of AI: A New Sigmoid Curve?" https://medium.com/geekculture/the-mass-adoption-of-ai-a-new-sigmoid-curve-c86cffe1617.

Scriven, Guy. 2023. "Generative AI Will Go Mainstream in 2024." https://www.economist.com/the-world-ahead/2023/11/13/generative-ai-will-go-mainstream-in-2024.

Swaner, Lynn E. and Rian Djita. 2024. *Navigating AI in Christian Schools*. Colorado Springs, CO: ACSI and Hamilton, ON: Cardus.

Part II: Christian School Perspectives

Chapter 4: The Head of School Perspective

Rispens, Skylar. "More College Students Using ChatGPT to Supplement Learning, Report Finds." October 4, 2023. https://edscoop.com/mcgraw-hill-survey-chatgpt-social-media/.

The Week. 2023. "Artificial Intelligence Goes to School: AI Is Transforming Education from Grade School to Grad School and Making Take-Home Essays Obsolete." *The Week*, August 12, 2023. https://theweek.com/education/1025698/artificial-intelligence-goes-to-school.

Chapter 5: The Teacher Perspective

Bailey, Ronald and Marian L. Tupy. 2020. *Ten Global Trends Every Smart Person Should Know: And Many Others You Will Find Interesting*. Washington, D.C.: Cato Institute.

Bordoloi, Satyen K. 2023. "The Hilarious and Horrifying Hallucinations of AI." February 7, 2023. https://www.sify.com/ai-analytics/the-hilarious-and-horrifying-hallucinations-of-ai/.

Bratt, James. 1998. *Abraham Kuyper: A Centennial Reader*. Grand Rapids, MI: Eerdmans.

FAO (Food and Agriculture Organization) of the United Nations. 2010. "Global Hunger Declining, but Still Unacceptably High." https://www.fao.org/4/al390e/al390e00.pdf.

Fowler, Geoffrey A. 2023. "Snapchat Tried to Make a Safe AI. It Chats with Me About Booze and Sex." https://www.washingtonpost.com/technology/2023/03/14/snapchat-myai/.

Hamilton, Arran, Dylan Wiliam, and John Hattie. 2023. "The Future of AI in Education: 13 Things We Can Do to Minimize the Damage." https://osf.io/preprints/edarxiv/372vr.

Lewis, Laurie. 2019. *Organizational Change: Creating Change Through Strategic Communication,* 2nd ed. New York: John Wiley & Sons.

Mansaray, Hassan Elsan. 2019. "The Role of Leadership Style in Organisational Change Management: A Literature Review." *Journal of Human Resource Management* 7, no. 1: 18–31.

Postman, Neil. 1998. "Five Things We Need to Know About Technological Change." Speech given in Denver, Colorado. March 28, 1998.

Postman, Neil. 1995. *The End of Education: Redefining the Value of School*. New York: Knopf.

Reinke, Tony. 2022. *God, Technology, and the Christian Life*. Wheaton, IL: Crossway.

Schuurman, Derek C. 2017. "Technology and the Biblical Story." *Pro Rege* 46, no. 1: 4–11.

References

Smith, Paul. 2023. "AI Glitter Fails to Decorate Snapchat's Slapdash Sentience." https://www.afr.com/technology/ai-glitter-fails-to-decorate-snapchat-s-slapdash-sentience-20230427-p5d3tj.

Tolkien, J.R.R. 1954. *The Lord of the Rings: The Fellowship of the Ring*. United Kingdom: Allen & Unwin.

Walsh, Brian J. and J. Richard Middleton. 1984. *The Transforming Vision: Shaping a Christian World View*. Downers Grove, IL: IVP Academic.

Part III: Frameworks for Practice

Chapter 7: A Framework for Technology Integration in Christian Schools

Brooker, Shaun. 2016. *Hacking at Trees with Chainsaws: The Essential Guide to Using Technology Effectively in the Classroom*. Apple Books. https://books.apple.com/nz/book/hacking-at-trees-with-chainsaws/id998177676/.

Chun, Russell. 2023. "Faculty Forum: Learning with ChatGPT." https://www.aaup.org/article/faculty-forum-learning-chatgpt.

Puentedura, Ruben R. 2006. "Transformation, Technology, and Education." http://hippasus.com/resources/tte/.

Chapter 8: Digital Well-Being and the Christian School

Borgmann, Albert. 1984. *Technology and the Character of Contemporary Life: A Philosophical Inquiry*. Chicago: University of Chicago Press.

Haidt, Jon. 2023. "Social Media is a Major Cause of the Mental Illness Epidemic in Teen Girls. Here's the Evidence." February 22, 2023. https://www.afterbabel.com/p/social-media-mental-illness-epidemic.

Killingsworth, Sean. 2023. Quoted in Episode 194 of the *1000 Hours Outside Podcast*. Accessed September 18, 2023. https://www.1000hoursoutside.com/podcast/episode194.

Rolheiser, Ronald. 2014. *The Holy Longing: The Search for a Christian Spirituality*. New York: Crown.

Vaillant, George E. 2015. *Triumphs of Experience: The Men of the Harvard Grant Study*. Cambridge: Harvard University Press.

ABOUT THE AUTHORS

Shaun Brooker is the head of school at Hamilton Christian School, a K–12 school in New Zealand. Brooker has taught in and led schools in his home country of New Zealand, as well as in the Cayman Islands and England. In 2016, he was recognized by Apple for his implementation of technology in education as an Apple Distinguished Educator, and two years later, the school he was leading became the first in New Zealand to be recognized as an Apple Distinguished Program. He served on an advisory board for Apple across Southeast Asia for three years. His greatest passion is not the potential of technology in education; it is the potential of Christian education and the opportunities within it to transform young lives. Much of Brooker's content can be viewed at www.christianeducation.org.nz.

Christina Crook is a pioneer and leading voice in digital well-being. The award-winning author of *The Joy of Missing Out: Finding Balance in a Wired World* (New Society Publishers) and *Good Burdens: How to Live Joyfully in a Digital Age* (Nimbus Publishing Ltd.), Crook now leads JOMO (campus), a digital wellness company serving college and high school students across North America. Crook is a Certified Digital Wellness Educator and sits on the board of *Second Nature Journal*, a publication of the International Institute of the Study of Technology and Christianity. She also is a harbinger of the global #JOMO movement and a member of the International Society for Technology in Education, the Media Ecology Association, Student Affairs Administrators in Higher Education (NASPA), and the Writers' Union of Canada.

Dr. Rian Djita is the director of research at the Association of Christian Schools International. He received his PhD from the Department of Education Reform at the University of Arkansas, where his dissertation topic focused on immigrant/first-generation college students and their postsecondary outcomes. He is a first-generation college student from Indonesia, where he taught high school math for six years. He earned his master's degree in international education policy at Peabody Vanderbilt with a Fulbright scholarship. During graduate school, he interned at the Tennessee Department of Education and the Center for Public Research and Leadership at Columbia University. He

About the Authors

was selected as one of the Emerging Education Policy Scholars (EEPS) in 2023. Djita's interests lie in comparative international policies around equity, international assessments, school choice, and students' academic outcomes, particularly among immigrant/English Language Learners (ELLs) and first-generation college students.

Dr. Scott Harsh assumed the role of president of Greater Atlanta Christian School (GAC) in 2018, becoming the third president in the school's more than fifty-year history. Before his appointment to president, he served at GAC since 1996 in various roles and responsibilities, including academic vice president, high school principal, high school dean of students, middle school assistant principal, as well as math teacher and coach of various sports. Harsh completed his bachelor's in mathematics from Harding University, his master's in educational leadership from the University of Georgia, an educational specialist degree from Georgia State University, and his doctoral degree in organizational leadership from Abilene Christian University. He also serves as chair of the board for the National Christian School Association.

Paul Matthews is an Australian educator who believes that Christian education is central to spreading God's kingdom throughout the world. He works with Christian schools to navigate the problems and possibilities of artificial intelligence in education. When not consulting or speaking, Matthews works as the CEO of MyTeacherAide, a tech start-up that helps bring the benefits of AI to teachers of all backgrounds and skill levels. He previously taught high school history at Calvin Christian School in Tasmania, Australia.

Dr. Dave Mulder currently serves as professor of education at Dordt University, where he teaches courses in educational technology, STEM education, and educational foundations. He previously served as a middle school math, science, and computer-science teacher in Christian schools in California and Iowa, and was technology director of a PreK–8 Christian school. He earned his doctoral degree in educational technology from Boise State University, and he continues to conduct research in digital citizenship, social presence in online learning, and technology integration in PreK–20 educational settings. He cohosts the *Hallway Conversations* podcast and provides professional development experiences for educators in schools across North America.

Dr. Derek C. Schuurman worked as an electrical engineer for several years and later completed a PhD at McMaster University in the area of robotics and computer vision using machine learning. He is currently professor of computer science at Calvin University, a fellow of the American Scientific Affiliation, and an advisor for AI and Faith. He has written about faith and technology issues in a variety of publications, including monthly columns in *Christian Courier* and contributions to the *Christian Scholar's Review* blog. He is the author of *Shaping a Digital World: Faith, Culture and Computer Technology* and co-author of *A Christian Field Guide to Technology for Engineers and Designers* (both IVP Academic).

Dr. Derek Wilson's current role is dean of technology and innovation at Greater Atlanta Christian School (GAC). At GAC, Wilson has worked on various projects, including synchronous learning; helping launch GAC's online school, Ethos; and providing professional development for schools across the United States. His current focus is developing TrekAI, an LLM-based tutor. Wilson's focus is on how to bring the best of technology into the classroom. His interests and skills are widespread with his doctoral work focusing on moral development psychology and bioethics education.

ABOUT THE SERIES EDITOR

Dr. Lynn E. Swaner is the president, U.S. at Cardus, a non-partisan think tank dedicated to clarifying and strengthening, through research and dialogue, the ways in which society's institutions can work together for the common good. She also serves as a senior fellow for the Association of Christian Schools International (ACSI) and a non-resident scholar at Baylor University's Center for School Leadership. Swaner is the editor or lead author of numerous books, including *Future Ready: Innovative Missions and Models in Christian Education* (Cardus & ACSI, 2022); *Flourishing Together: A Christian Vision for Students, Educators, and Schools* (Eerdmans, 2021); and *MindShift: Catalyzing Change in Christian Education* (ACSI, 2019). She previously served as a professor of education and a Christian school leader in New York, and she holds a doctorate in organizational leadership from Teachers College, Columbia University and a diploma in strategy and innovation from Saïd Business School at the University of Oxford.

More from Leading Insights

eBook available

ACSI Leading Insights Biblical Worldview and Spiritual Formation

This monograph, *Biblical Worldview and Spiritual Formation*, focuses on the core mission of Christian education—discipling the hearts and minds of students, and equipping them as ambassadors of Christ and reconcilers to God's creation. With chapters by leaders, teachers, and researchers who have worked extensively in and with Christian schools, this edition shares valuable insights for fostering a school culture that is rooted in a biblical worldview and love of God and neighbor. Practical strategies and a culminating reflection guide will benefit readers in any role—whether in leadership, spiritual life oversight, classroom teaching, curricular planning, faculty professional development, or service-learning—as well as school teams seeking to grow in faithfulness to their Christ-centered mission.

Books in the Leading Insights Series:
1. Special Education and Inclusion
2. Mental Health and Well-Being
3. Biblical Worldview and Spiritual Formation
4. Artificial Intelligence

Purchase at PurposefulDesign.com.

ACSI
STRONGER TOGETHER

It's Time to Flourish

For over 40 years, ACSI has been leading Christ-centered education toward excellence and continually seeking to understand what truly impacts and improves Christian schools. Through this mission, ACSI developed the Flourishing School Culture Model. Backed by rigorous research and God's Word, the Flourishing School Culture Model provides the framework to measure school community strengths and weaknesses to help your school create an action plan that results in cultural transformation. With tools and training, we are equipping you to leave a legacy for the students who sit in your classrooms. Through the Flourishing School Culture Model, you can assess, understand, and gain a new vision for your school's culture.

The Flourishing School Culture Model includes five domains that incorporate 35 validated constructs. Each domain provides clarity and context for interpreting and understanding flourishing in Christian schools.

To learn more about the Flourishing School Culture Model, visit **acsi.org/flourishing**.

It's time for your school culture to flourish!